Fostering Mixed Race Children

Fiona Peters

Fostering Mixed Race Children

Everyday Experiences of Foster Care

Fiona Peters
Goldsmiths, University of London
London, UK

ISBN 978-1-137-54183-3   ISBN 978-1-137-54184-0   (eBook)
DOI 10.1057/978-1-137-54184-0

Library of Congress Control Number: 2016941859

© The Editor(s) (if applicable) and The Author(s) 2016
The author(s) has/have asserted their right(s) to be identified as the author(s) of this work in accordance with the Copyright, Designs and Patents Act 1988.
This work is subject to copyright. All rights are solely and exclusively licensed by the Publisher, whether the whole or part of the material is concerned, specifically the rights of translation, reprinting, reuse of illustrations, recitation, broadcasting, reproduction on microfilms or in any other physical way, and transmission or information storage and retrieval, electronic adaptation, computer software, or by similar or dissimilar methodology now known or hereafter developed.
The use of general descriptive names, registered names, trademarks, service marks, etc. in this publication does not imply, even in the absence of a specific statement, that such names are exempt from the relevant protective laws and regulations and therefore free for general use.
The publisher, the authors and the editors are safe to assume that the advice and information in this book are believed to be true and accurate at the date of publication. Neither the publisher nor the authors or the editors give a warranty, express or implied, with respect to the material contained herein or for any errors or omissions that may have been made.

Printed on acid-free paper

This Palgrave Macmillan imprint is published by Springer Nature
The registered company is Macmillan Publishers Ltd.
The registered company address is: The Campus, 4 Crinan Street, London, N1 9XW, United Kingdom

Acknowledgements

There are many people who have kept me company on this journey—so many guides and helpers sent to show me, teach me, or force me to make a greater commitment to my life and my writing.

This book has been written in the hope that readers will open their minds and hearts and really feel what it means to live such a complex childhood in foster care, and to know that every young life deserves to have a childhood free from fear, worry, and anxiety. Children need to feel loved, safe, and secure so they are able to do what children do naturally—share joy, love, and laughter. Thank you to the Children's Social Care Department who participated in this research and the one amazing change-maker who made it all possible. Through sharing their lives, the young people in this book have changed my life, and perhaps they will change yours. They are brave, trusting, and honest and children like them must never be written off. Thank you Lucy, Ocean, Stealth, Amma, Jasmine, and Tallulah.

To my parents who were my first guides in love and tenacity and who raised me to be fearless—I love you. Thank you. Caroline and Hazel— thank you for your acceptance and love. To Chevon, Conrad, Anthea, Bianca, and Andrew, who have lived with uncertainty and persevered, and to Kyra, Rihana, Aleesha, Tian, Leila, Anthony, and Marco, who only know love and stability—words cannot express how happy you all make me.

For Bernadette Roden—I wish I could show you this book. I am forever indebted. For Michelle 'Midge'—Chloé will be forever changed by knowing you.

My champions are: Dr Chamion Cabellero for her support on this project; Dr Deirdre Osborne for always being for alerting me to opportunities; Paul Halliday for creative inspiration; Professor Caroline Knowles for valuing the study of family; and Bridget Ward for caring deeply. Thank you to my dearest friends who are patient, wise, grounding, supportive, and fun. I acknowledge the assistance provided by the Economic and Social Research Council and the Sociology Department at Goldsmiths during the writing of this book. I appreciate the numerous professional connections and conversations that emerged during the writing of this book as well as the random incidents that put me on new paths of exploration.

Thank you to my family who have supported this book: my daughter Rochelle, my intellectual warrior, friend, and nurturer who inspires me; my daughter Chloé, my guide, focus, friend, and motivational coach; my son Finlay, for showing his phenomenal work ethic and reminding me to crack on; and my baby Isis for being so full of joy that makes me know all is well. You are ALL my greatest achievements. Jason my best friend and support car—the sun continues to shine!

Contents

List of Figures

1

Care Matters and Mixed Race Children

Mixed race children are known to have adverse care experiences and those of white and black Caribbean or African heritage are more likely to be in care than any other ethnic group. The UK Censuses from 2001 and 2011 revealed that the mixed ethnic group almost doubled during this period. Further, the 2011 Census shows almost 50 % of all mixed people are under the age of sixteen. The confusion over how to classify and place mixed children for fostering has been subject to intense academic and practitioner debate in relation to ethnic matching and same race placements. Children looked after are primarily living in foster placements, but the carer shortage impacts on the types of placements and quality of care available. Notions of identity, culture, ethnicity, and race are all played out in the politicized site of Children's Social Care. Within the local authority where the research for this book took place, the guidelines surrounding matching suggest that children 'do not stand out as visibly different' to the foster family. However, this undermines the social legitimacy of mixed families for whom visible difference is ordinary. Mixedness is understood as a problematic identification and has been theorized within the dominant psychologizing notions of identity without attention to the wider social processes of race-making. This book aims

© The Editor(s) (if applicable) and The Author(s) 2016
F. Peters, *Fostering Mixed Race Children*,
DOI 10.1057/978-1-137-54184-0_1

to examine structural inequalities in decision-making by exploring how mixed race children's everyday lives become underpinned by racialization practices in Children's Social Care.

The narratives of children and young people currently experiencing foster care offer rich and insightful knowledge about how they make meaning of their lives. Using a form of participatory research, photographs and images supplied from the family album underpin and enhance the narratives, and each case study is presented as a separate chapter ranging from care admission to care leaving. The two central questions underpinning the research are: How do children and young people derive meaning from the discursive repertoires of the mixed classification in their care experiences? In what ways are foster care experiences being structured through understandings of mixedness?

The four case studies in the book are organized around a fairly typical care trajectory. Firstly, care admission during which race, culture, and ethnic belonging underpin appropriate placements. Secondly, long-term foster care, when decisions about permanence can be hampered by same race matching guidelines. Thirdly, short-term foster care, when belonging within distinct racial, ethnic, and cultural categories can lead to transience and instability. Finally, a discussion of how the circumstances upon leaving the care support system or entering semi-independent living demonstrate that mixed race as a social location (when linked to gender, sexuality, age, and geographical location) can lead to increased sexual exploitation and vulnerability for female care leavers.

The material is theoretically informed and policy relevant and makes a contribution to sociological and practitioner knowledge regarding mixedness as a classification and category used to organize lives. It pays attention to ongoing debates concerning mixed as both an ethnic and racial category and the development of this category for official population counts.

The content of the book introduces a number of key concerns in relation to how mixed race families are understood in Children's Social Care through a sociological analysis of race, class, gender, geographical location, and sexuality. It explores mixed as a classification with ambiguous and uncertain ethnic, cultural, and racial boundaries, which leads to inconsistent decision-making among practitioners.

Chapter Outlines

Chapter 2, 'Fostering Mixed Race Children', explores the image and function of care from its philanthropic beginnings to the state-controlled bureaucracy administering foster care that is prevalent today. Care is a transclass and transrace institution, and mixed race children are caught up in ongoing debates over appropriate ethnic and racial socialization, yet care matching guidelines do not specifically consider their mixed heritage. Subsequently, confusion is a characteristic of practitioner decision-making and mixed children's care experiences are underpinned by inconsistent interpretation of guidelines.

Chapter 3, 'Conceptualization and Categorization of Mixedness', examines mixedness as an ethnic group in England and Wales with attention to US influences. By examining existing data and research on adverse care experiences it demonstrates that mixedness is a disadvantage at all stages of care assessment and intervention. Understanding practitioner assumptions about mixed families and the intersection of class, gender, sexuality, and race is an important factor in mitigating high care admission rates of mixed children. The language and terminology to describe mixed people remains contestable and do not easily lead to constructing a sense of belonging across racial or ethnic boundaries. However, commonality of lived experience is possible within this internally diverse ethnic and racial group.

Chapter 4, 'Researching Mixedness as a Category of Experience', outlines the theoretical implications of researching mixedness and the racialization practices within research and Children's Social Care. It pays methodological attention to developing participation and working with vulnerable young people, and acknowledges the role of emotional research and emotions in research. The data collection began as a project funded by the Economic and Social Research Council (ESRC). The use of everyday experience and narrative leads to qualitative data, which is often beyond the themes of the research agenda and opens up new areas of sociological enquiry.

Chapter 5, 'The First Year in Care and the Matrix of Classifications', is the first case study and examines care admission through the narrative of the only boy in the project—Stealth. Dealing with the loss of his family life, Stealth's first year in care outlines how same race matching does not always mean ethnic sameness. His mixed classification is outside of the fifty/fifty binary with which mixedness is commonly understood, and his negotiation of securing a legitimate label and identification shifts according to space and time. The collapse of race, culture, and ethnicity is made apparent during his first year in care and he questions his belonging to his foster family. There is a discussion of how the construction of childhoods in foster care are far from ordinary and present Stealth with bureaucratic limitations on his everyday experience of childhood.

Chapter 6, 'Family Ties Through the Lens', examines the narratives of Jasmine and Tallulah, sisters who have been in long-term foster care for nine years. Through their family album they delve into memory, loyalty, and belonging and show the different ways they understand their care experiences. It examines how widespread assumptions about inter racial relationships influence the decisions made by social care, consequently inhibiting the siblings stability for long term care with a white foster care. This chapter explores assumptions surrounding the role of white mothering of mixed race children and suggests this may continue to be a factor in both high rates of care admission and long-term stability with white foster carers.

Chapter 7, 'A Portrait of Transience Through Care', follows Amma as she uses photography to explore her past and revisit people and places. Her care journey is one of transience and she has been in almost twenty varied placements during her six years in care. She finds belonging through notions of diaspora and links to familial identities and ethnic heritages, speaking through discourses of class and location. The matching processes to place her result in separation from her three siblings and movement through a range of ethnic, racial, and cultural placements where she becomes chameleon-like in her adaptation to her new environments.

Chapter 8, 'The Leaving Care Transition', introduces Lucy as she leaves care with her baby daughter. Her narrative construction enables an understanding of how she performs her mixedness—as she is subject to misrecognition—and this slippage requires further anchoring through an ethnic performance to secure a contestable racial identification. The construction of mixedness, gender, and age makes her vulnerable to sexual exploitation in specific public spaces. However, she uses her sexual desirability in remarkable ways to secure greater social capital through her choice of dating partners and motherhood.

Chapter 9, 'Learning from Mixed Race Children in Foster Care', suggests children's views on the here and now have largely been ignored. Paying attention to how children understand racialization within foster care offers rich knowledge to improve service delivery and advance theorization of mixedness as a lived experience. It offers conclusions in relation to the importance of developing greater awareness of the pressures faced by mixed families and the development of services and support during early intervention. Tackling assumptions about mixed families is a crucial step towards mitigating consistently high rates of care admission and offering mixed families a socially legitimate space. Through acknowledgement that mixed families appear visibly different, Children's Social Care can prioritize the emotional and attachment needs of children. Matching processes for fostering need revision to account for cultural customs within the child's birth family by prioritizing their primary socialization rather than crude applications of ethnic and racial classification. The adverse care experiences and high rates of admission suggest that mixed race children of white and black Caribbean or African heritage need specific assessment to deliver services appropriate to need.

2

Fostering Mixed Race Children

Children's Social Care is in the midst of an institutional crisis. Solutions are being sought to re-work the image and function of foster care where 75% of all children looked after live. Often children remain vulnerable in birth families, as practitioners are reluctant to take them into care because of its institutional failings—care is seen as a last resort. A revaluation of care is long overdue in order to re-cast it as a positive alternative for struggling families and a safe and suitable place for young people that works in their best interests. Gentleman confirms

> The state's inability to provide adequate care for some of the country's neediest children is one of Britain's most acute social injustices ... many things remain very wrong with the system: poorly trained workers in front-line positions, high staff turnover and a chronic shortage of foster parents, so that children are not carefully matched with suitable carers but placed wherever is available. (20/04/2009)

The statistical first release offers national and local data on outcomes for children looked after continuously for twelve months. The figures are based on those collected annually through the longitudinal children looked after return or SSDA903 completed by all local authorities in England. In

© The Editor(s) (if applicable) and The Author(s) 2016   **7**
F. Peters, *Fostering Mixed Race Children*,
DOI 10.1057/978-1-137-54184-0_2

2016 the educational attainment of looked after children shows five or more GCSE's at A*-C is at 14%, an increase on 2015's 12%. However, children in care are twice as likely to be permanently excluded from school as are all children. Sixty one per cent of children looked after have a special educational need compared to 15% of all children. They are three times more likely to have a primary need of social, emotional, and mental health and less likely to have speech and language problems (DfE, 2015).

Further data shows the numbers of children looked after is steadily increasing and up 5% from 2012 and at 70,440 of which 74% (51,850) live with foster carers.

Based on data collected for the first time in 2016 and released as experimental statistics (to be treated with caution) 10% of 17-year-old care leavers were recorded as being in custody, higher than for older care leavers where the figure was 3% for 18 year olds, and 4% for 19, 20, and 21 year olds. Forty per cent of care levers were not in education, employment, or training compared to 12% of all other young people. Interestingly, the increase was in the category for NEET due to illness or disability and NEET due to pregnancy or parenting (DfE, 2016).

Very little research is done with children currently in foster care and this book sets out to address this gap in knowledge. As C. Wright Mills suggested in The Sociological Imagination, '[n]either the life of an individual nor the history of a society can be understood without understanding both' (2000 [1959]: 3). The overwhelming critique of care among both professionals and young people to emerge from consultations and the government report by the House of Commons (McLeod 2008) suggests that care fails to deliver the kind of warmth, stability, security, or love that young people deserve and ought to expect. Channel 4 television documentary, *Dispatches*, conducted an undercover investigation into the Surrey Children and Families Social Work Department which demonstrated that young people between the ages of twelve and sixteen are let down, left behind, and ignored by an over-stretched care system (*Dispatches* 2010). Society positions young children in care as being at risk of abuse. They occupy front-page news, mostly when they fail to be protected by effective communication between the key child protection agencies. Children in care have been and are targets for sexual and physical abuse by staff in residential children's homes. They become silent victims because of their age, vulnerability, and need for adult protection. Adolescents occupy the position of rebellious, feral, and out of control youth, perpetrators of crime and drug abuse. They are seen as failures and potential social misfits. This polarized dynamic of risk to and risk from children in care feeds into their construction of childhood in social life. Research with children in care seeks to understand how the institution of foster care functions in the here and now and the impact this has on ordinary lived experience.

In Britain children and young people are designated as people in their own right, yet their freedom to exercise choices is limited by arbitrary legal restrictions on everything from drinking alcohol to the age at which they can marry or join the army. The limitation of choice and lack of freedom to exercise rights renders young people dependent on adults (Christensen and O'Brien 2003). The boundaries of the adult/young person relationship become challenged when young people are in care; firstly, they are separated from their families and can no longer depend (if they ever have been able to) on that adult relationship, and secondly, adult professionals such as carers and social workers who take on the role of substitute parent can potentially be (and often are) undependable due to the pressures, processes, and constraints of working in a care system in crisis.

Saving children from moral, physical, and spiritual decline has its beginnings in socio-political actions of philanthropist Thomas Coram who set up the first Victorian children's home. At the time children were both living and dying on the streets in Britain, perhaps cared for by private individuals or in institutions under punitive regimes of control. Only later did state intervention insist that local authorities become responsible for children in their vicinity. The 1908 Children and Young Persons Act had one central aim, to protect children from harm by removing them from home when the risks of leaving them there were greater. Subsequent amendments of 1948 and 1989 had the same goal of removal, showing deference to an untested model of public care (Ritchie 2005: 3). Evidence-based research suggests, firstly, that at no time was there an assessment of the effectiveness of care through child removal, and secondly, that the outcomes of care leavers point to a system flawed and dogged by institutional failures and professionals lacking adequate training and support in caring for the country's most vulnerable children and young people (Ibid.: 3).

The Emergence and Use of Fostering

Research by Bowlby (1953) post World War II suggested that poor behaviour and the delinquency of children and young people in residential care was due to maternal deprivation as they lacked a warm one-to-one relationship. Foster care became increasingly popular and attempts to replicate the ecology of the family were ushered in, bolstered by the Curtis Report of 1946 and The Children Act of 1948 for Fostering. Both asserted that fostering in families should be privileged over residential care. During the 1980s residential care use began to decline sharply, and there was an increasing focus on permanence and strategies to reduce the drift and poor achievements and outcomes of care leavers. This was in addition to the anti-institutional thinking led by Goffman (1963), which made the economics and ideology of foster care attractive to social services departments (Stein 1999). However, there are simply not enough foster families for the increase in children being cared for by local authorities: '[t]he current shortage of foster carers means that children in crisis are all too often placed in any free bed, rather than with the most suitable foster family. If these children are going to have the same opportunities in life as other children then we need to invest in a foster care service fit for the 21st century' (Collier 2010).

Improving the image of fostering to both enlarge and improve the quality of carers focuses on initiatives such as guaranteed minimum fostering allowances, structured training programmes and the opportunity to work in partnership with childcare professionals (BAAF 2010). The National Minimum Fostering Allowances have been set in order to reflect age differences, with higher rates for London and the South East. Rates among private agencies can be as much as £400–£500 per child per week depending on age. The emergence of fostering as the best form of care for children who can no longer live at home is now in crisis due to the shortage and the quality of care, as children and young people fail to find suitable long-term matches or are moved through a series of short-term placements.

It is known that as of 2015 The Fostering Network suggests there is a shortage of over eight thousand foster carers needed for increasing numbers of children. Figures from CoramBAAF suggest approximately seventy thousand children are in care each year. Seventy-five per cent are in foster homes, 9% in residential or secure homes, 3% are in community placement, and 3% in residential schools. Fifty-five per cent are boys, 45% are girls, 38% are between the ages of ten and fifteen years, 77% are white, 9% have a mixed racial background, 7% are black, and 4% are Asian. Seventy-five per cent of all children in care are seen as 'hard to place', characterized as over the age of five years; Black Minority Ethnic (BME); disabled; or a sibling group (http://corambaaf.org.uk/res/statengland). What is also clear is the nature of foster care has evolved over fifty years. 'Foster care offers a diverse service, the commonest form is short term, less than three months in keeping with the ideology in both the US and the UK that foster care is not parenting, and that almost all children are best off with their biological parents' (Minty 1999).

The privatization of foster care remains polarized by class stratification as poorer children are usually fostered into materially better-off families. Class stratification informs the regulation and standardization of parenting through state-led initiatives (Barn 2007) which allow professionals to judge parents against objective criteria of hygiene, supervision, and nutrition. 'Concerns of child protection are very specific; they evaluate risk to the child in terms of parenting rather than in terms of poverty' (Ritchie 2005: 2). Gillies (2007) concurs that parenting standards centre middle-class values and whiteness as normative, which excludes practices specific to working-class and ethnic minority parents and marginalizes their experiences. Those excluded from increasingly normative and legitimate middle-class values are subject to state intervention remedies to address exclusion, 'orientated towards re-attaching the afflicted through the modification of their lifestyle and conduct' (ibid.: 23).

Cohen (1994: 48) confirms: '[t]ransclass placements, which continue to be the norm, have always been articulated to discourses of "race" and nation. It is only recently that black people in Britain have become their main focus'. Discourses of nation in British welfare intervention have rested upon the articulation of Britishness to whiteness and deeming 'other' cultures inferior and in need of civilizing.

Transrace Versus Same Race Fostering

The cultural deficit model based on Eurocentric standards judged black and mixed families as lacking in the appropriate skills to raise their children within notions of shared national values. Up until the 1980s, the practices of care admission for large numbers of black British African-Caribbean and mixed children relied on this model (Barn 1993). Caribbean children were removed from families due to assumptions about dysfunctional family forms; in particular, matriarchal family structures were misunderstood. The high numbers of black children in residential care did not direct attention to *why* they were in care but rather were complicit with the pathologization of black family life. Causal factors of care admission were never fully investigated. As Gilroy (1994: xi) notes, 'racism itself should be recognized as a factor in increasing household stresses and conflicts about money, status and power, gender and generations'. Reasons behind such large numbers of black and mixed children's care admissions rested upon a willingness to accept black pathology as a way to understand all black families, which included the experiences of mixed children who were then considered black both in social work practice and in social life (Banks 1992, 1995; Maximé 1993; Prevatt-Goldstein 1999; Small 1986). This position led to an easy acceptance of high numbers of black (and mixed) children in care and the assumed cultural benefits of transracial fostering and adoption. During the 1980s, underpinned by support from the Association of Black Social Workers and Allied Professionals (ABSWAP) and cultural relativism, new approaches stated that all cultures were to be seen as equal and this strategy established a more anti-oppressive practice.

Through the underpinning of cultural relativism and anti-oppressive practice, practitioners began to oppose transracial adoption and fostering (placing black and mixed children with white families). Debates used the language of race—identity stripping, assimilation, cultural hegemony, authentic black identity, confusion, and survival techniques for racism—to describe the experiences of those transracially adopted and fostered. The ABSWAP gathered support for opposing all transracial adoptions and fostering practices, bringing their objections and solutions to the House of Commons Select Committee to support a same race policy, arguing that 'black children should be placed exclusively with black families' (Tizard and Phoenix 1993: 89). Mixed children were never considered separately from black children. Despite being embedded within their white maternal families it was assumed that mixed children ought to be seen as black and racialized into one of the two available classifications and thus they were placed as black in the care system.

Often no distinction was made between children with one black parent and those with two black parents (Small 1986). The adage that mixed people are black, because that is how society sees them, has been considered worthy of critical attention and deconstruction by mixed race studies (Dewan 2008; Olumide 2002; Root 1989; Song 2003). Within social work literature concerning hard to place black children (de Sousa and Simmonds 2007; Gaber 1994), mixed children were included but rarely explicitly so (Tizard and Phoenix 1993). Public services discourse and more specifically Children's Social Care could consider more carefully that there is a mixed race perspective as Morley and Street (2014: 67) assert: 'Following the one drop rule is no longer acceptable but is a default position'. The increasing attention paid to and inclusion of mixed as an ethnic category in England and Wales and racial classification in the USA has led to an examination of mixedness as a distinct category and to greater attention to the mixed experience, an outcome of which is greater knowledge of the consistently high numbers and adverse experiences of children in care.

As policy and guidelines moved away from transracial adoption and fostering, 'race, became the principle factor for matching and bonding in families' (Cohen 1994: 59). However, Gilroy (1994: xi) argues, 'cultural sameness and common bodily characteristics do not, by themselves, promote good parenting'. The sweeping generalizations made about the dysfunctional nature of black families and the authenticity of their ability to promote culture are two sides of the same coin; both lack interrogation of black family forms and treat the black family as homogeneous. Currently the policy of same race matching remains in practice within local authority foster care placement guidelines. The confusion over how to racially classify mixed children and young people and select the appropriate placement reflects a lack of critical attention paid to their identification practices and their family background, and it also reflects the lack of attention paid to the heterogeneous nature of black and mixed family forms.

Fostering and Mixed Race Children

Foster placements for mixed children within a climate of same race matching, in conjunction with the foster carer shortage, means that, for the most part, mixed children wait longer for a potential match, during which time they are often placed in short-term placements not always appropriate to need (Thoburn 2005: 118). In practice the placements thought suitable for mixed young people often include white carers as a preference as this reflects the birth family, although they are not always thought to be suitable for long-term fostering. These assertions have their basis in arguments about cultural reproduction and appropriate socialization. Social workers often have a shortage of black carers and mixed young people do not get priority of need in relation to culture and ethnicity. Thoburn and colleagues (2000a, b) examined foster placements and the attitudes of the children and their carers over the time of the placement. The findings suggest that the families, even if two parents were white, became mixed upon the arrival of the foster child, which raised race awareness as 'all the families empathized with the issues around visible difference and racism' (2000a, b: 12). Findings suggested that race, ethnicity, faith, and culture had a bearing on how integration into the new family was negotiated with the child (Thoburn 2000a: 122). The overall conclusion states that 'some white families can successfully meet the needs of children of mixed parentage, especially if they live in ethnically mixed communities' (ibid: 123). The ongoing controversy surrounding the classification and categorizations of mixed children is fraught with politically entrenched positions among social work practitioners who are aware of cultural needs and fearful their abandonment (as has happened in adoption) will see a return to high levels of transrace fostering of the past.

However, recruitment of African and Caribbean foster families for the purposes of same race matching operates under the enduring legacy of research done by Wilson (1987). She discovered that 'it is not enough for prospective parents to be black, they must also feel good about being black and be able to transmit that feeling to the child' (1987: ix). Such cultural bias during assessment demonstrates the assumption that white families automatically feel good about their whiteness. The dissonance between how white and black families are assessed for their suitability as foster parents would deter some Caribbean and African families who, given the consequences of discrimination, do find their ethnic heritage challenging. How families can be measured in relation to 'feeling good about being black' is unknown, but it may account for the low recruitment levels of black foster carers.

Mixed Race Care, Transience, and Resilience

Research shows that mixed children and young people in care experience two types of disruption to home life: firstly, moving from one foster family to another and secondly, changes in geographical location and schools (Barn et al. 2005). Finding suitable matches for mixed children and the shortage of carers results in movement through a series of short-term foster placements (Thoburn et al. 2000a, b). 'The upheaval of home, carers, schools, and geographical location has implications for trust, a sense of belonging and impacts on young people's relationships' (Barn 2010: 10). Trust is critical in understanding young people who experience instability (Oosterman et al. 2006). Movement and disruption, which are a result of placement breakdowns and result in unplanned moves, can often 'be experienced as another relationship failure and rejection' (Frost et al. 1999: 117). There is a complex relationship between stability and good outcomes, so individual personality or educational success may contribute to stability in a placement, despite transience also being a feature of their care experience. Barn's findings confirm that: '[i]n terms of placements with foster carers which reflected the young people's racial and cultural background … mixed parentage conveyed a history of placement disruption and the instability caused by this' (Barn 2010: 10).

Decision-making among practitioners, which asserts mixedness or race as a factor to move children from placements where they do not appear to be appropriately ethnically or racially matched, can often obscure how children themselves understand the role and priority of racial identification in their own lives. It is significant to note that research among young people in higher education indicates that '[r]acial identity is not a master identity … and includes ethnic, national, cultural and religions affiliations' (Aspinall and Song 2013: 184). That is not to throw the baby out with the bath water and suggest 'race' is no longer important, but it is one factor among many others that need to be given due consideration. Barn and colleagues (2005: 5) suggest that 'local authorities actively seek to avoid disruption and instability to avoid social exclusion and accumulative disadvantage in the lives of young people' since such instability is thought to precipitate poor post-care experiences. Mixed young people experience such comparatively high rates of disruption and instability that their disadvantages in all areas of concern are markedly greater than for other ethnic groups (Barn et al. 2005).

Children's Social Care places emphasis on overcoming transience by building resilience in children and young people, rather than an engagement with the policy and practice decisions that engender transience. Resilience is deemed 'the quality that enables some young people to find fulfilment in their lives despite their disadvantaged backgrounds … it is about overcoming the odds, coping and recovery' (Stein 2005: 264). Resilience and protective factors are the positive side of risk and vulnerability both within the child and the care system. Considerations of intelligence, temperament, and education, in addition to caring adults, good schools, and high expectations, make some children more resilient than others (ibid.: 264). However, a focus on the resilience of the child omits an engagement with the very practices that make the concept of resilience a pre-requisite for children in care. While resilience is an essential life skill, its over-application negates poor practice and burdens children in care with the responsibility for overcoming what can be dire circumstances.

Care Leavers

Research shows that young people in stable placements are more likely to be successful in education and work, as care leavers, and become socially integrated than those who experience movement and disruption

(Barn et al. 2005; Biehal and Wade 1996; Stein 2005). Outcomes-based research on care leavers shows them to be one of the most disadvantaged groups in society. The National Audit Office concluded that '[t]he poor life experiences of too many care leavers are a long-standing problem. Without well targeted support their deep needs will not be met, with costly consequences for the young people and for society' (Care Leavers Transition to Adulthood 2015). They have poor educational outcomes, are less likely to be in post-sixteen education, experience high unemployment, homelessness, mental health problems, and young parenthood, and engage in risk-taking behaviours such as criminal activity and drug use (Barn et al. 2005; Biehal and Wade 1996; Stein 1999). They leave care at an average age of seventeen—much earlier than those not in care. Research shows that young care leavers who have experience of stable placements are more likely to be successful in education and work than those who experience movement and disruption. Any support they receive from foster carers is due to goodwill rather than any secure official arrangement (Barn 2010). The government initiative 'Staying Put' allows them to stay with foster carers until age twenty-one but they can, and often do, choose to leave much earlier. Preparation for leaving care is now implemented through the Children (Leaving Care) Act 2000, which outlines pathway planning to include discussions with young people about impending independence and to move them on in similar ways to other young people, ideally in a more protracted and supported way.

Research findings show that care leavers feel rushed, disappointed, and forced to make unsuitable choices of accommodation (Barn 2010; Stein 1999). Their choices often leave them lonely and isolated with poor networks in the community and little by way of educational or employment opportunities (Barn 2010). The first two years out of care can result in further disruption as '[a] half make two or more moves and a sixth make five or more moves, as well as one fifth becoming homeless' (Stein 1999: 121). In 2009 figures show that 25 % of all homeless young people had been in care. The poor planning and support and the fast changes are found to be disempowering for young people and lead to adverse experiences around budgeting, tenancies, and employment.

Statistics collated by the National Audit Office (2015) in their report 'Care Leavers' Transition to Adulthood' suggests that every year almost ten thousand young people between the ages of sixteen and eighteen leave care. Of these, 6% go on to higher education and are supported until the age of twenty-five. During 2013–2014, 49% were NEETs (Not in Education, Employment or Training). Almost 49% of males in the criminal justice system have been in care. Twenty-two per cent of girls leaving care are pregnant. Care leavers are four to five times more likely to self-harm than other young people.

Ofsted began an inspection programme in 2013 and found that across fifty-nine local authority Care Leaving Services only 34% were rated as 'good'. Local authorities do not keep in touch with their care leavers beyond the age of twenty-one. Only eight out of 151 local authorities reported that they knew where all their care leavers were living and whether they were in employment or training. Further, the Department of Education does not collect data on care leavers beyond the age of twenty-one. The system is acknowledged to be patchy and inconsistent and relies on voluntary organizations to plug the gap in services. A recent conference in Manchester run by the Care Leavers' Association (2010) consulted care leavers, and their findings suggest that greater support to achieve independence through help with budgeting, housing, education, careers, and life skills would make the transition from care to care leaver smoother.

Corporate parenting, as the entire care system is now known, is an institutional framework of agencies and professionals with specific responsibilities and a duty of care for children who cannot be looked after by their birth families. The care of children looked after by the local authority is currently a concern of big business, government, and charities. The 'Care Matters' government white paper, issued in June 2007, aims to deliver improved services to young people in care. Beverley Hughes, the former Labour government Children's Minister, states: '[t]here is a significant gap between the quality of life and future prospects of children in care and those of other children' (Hughes 2008). Quality of life includes physical, health, social, educational, and emotional well-being (NICE 2015, 2016. See references). If care and more specifically foster care remains the option of choice for children looked after, more needs to be known about its users and their perception of care and the impact of its failings on their lives. What we do know about mixed children in care offers a bleak statistical picture, however, and knowledge of their everyday lives is limited. In order to reveal the impact of a mixed classification on fostering experiences, corporate parenting must be examined through racialization processes during a typical care trajectory.

References

Aspinall, P. J., & Song, M. (2013). *Mixed race identities*. Basingstoke: Palgrave Macmillan.

Banks, N. (1992). Techniques for direct work with Black children. *Fostering and Adoption, 16*(3), 19–25.

Banks, N. (1995). Children of Black mixed parentage and their placement needs. *Fostering and Adoption, 19*(2), 19–24.

Barn, R. (1993). *Black children in the public care system*. London: Batsford.

Barn, R. (2007). 'Race', ethnicity and child welfare: A fine balancing act. *British Journal of Social Work, 37*(8), 1425–1434.

Barn, R. (2010). Care leavers and social capital: Understanding and negotiating racial and ethnic identity. *Ethnic and Racial Studies, 33*(5), 832–850. (Special Issue: Young People, Ethnicity and Social Capital).

Barn, R., Andrew, L., & Mantovani, N. (2005). *Life after care: A study of the experiences of young people from different ethnic groups*. York: Joseph Rowntree Foundation.

Biehal, N., Clayden, J., Stein, M., & Wade, J. (1992). *Prepared for living? A survey of young people leaving the care of three local authorities*. London: National Children's Bureau.

Biehal, N., & Wade, J. (1996). Looking back, looking forward: Care leavers, families and change. *Children and Youth Services Review, 18*(4–5), 425–445.

Bowlby, J. (1953). *Child care and the growth of love*. Baltimore, MD: Pelican Books.

Christensen, P., & O'Brien, M. (Eds.), (2003). *Children in the city: Home, neighbourhood and community*. London: RoutledgeFalmer.

Cohen, P. (1994). Yesterday's words, tomorrow's world: From the racialisation of adoption to the politics of difference. In I. Gaber & J. Aldridge (Eds.), *Culture, identity and transracial adoption: In the best interests of the child*. London: Free Association Books.

De Sousa, S., & Simmonds, J. (2007). *Judgement of Solomon*. Paper given at Mixedness and Mixing conference. British Association of Adoption and Fostering.

Dewan, I. A. (2008). *Recasting race: Women of mixed heritage in further education.* Stoke-on-Trent: Trentham Books.

DfE. (2015). *Outcomes for children looked after by local authorities in England in 2015.* Department for Education, SFR11/2016, 24 March 2016.

DfE. (2016). *Children looked after in England (including adoption) year ending* 31 March 2016-12-01, SFR 41/2016 29 September 2016.

Finlayson, N. (2009). In A. Gentlemen (Ed.), Children in care: How Britain is failings its most vulnerable. *The Guardian.* https://www.theguardian.com/society/2009/ apr/20/care-system-failures

Frost, N., Mills, S., & Stein, M. (1999). *Understanding residential child care.* Aldershot: Ashgate.

Gentleman, A. (2009). Children in care: How Britain is failing its most vulnerable. *The Guardian.* https://www.theguardian.com/society/2009/apr/20/care-system-failures

Gillies, V. (2007). *Marginalised mothers: Exploring working-class experiences of parenting.* London: Routledge.

Gilroy, P. (1994). cited in Kirton, D. (2000). *'Race', ethnicity and adoption.* Buckingham: Open University Press.

Goffman, E. (1963). *Stigma: Notes on the management of spoiled identity.* London: Penguin.

Maximé, J. (1993). The importance of racial identity for the psychological well-being of Black children. *Association for Child Psychology and Psychiatry Review and Newsletter, 15*(4), 173–179.

McLeod, A. (2008). *Listening to children: A practitioner's guide.* London: Jessica Kingsley.

Minty, B. (1999). Outcome in long term family foster care. *Journal of Child Psychiatry, 30*(7/Oct), 991–999.

Morley, D., & Street, C. (2014). *Mixed experiences: Mental health and well-being.* London: National Children's Bureau.

Olumide, J. (2002). *Raiding the gene pool: The social construction of mixed race.* London: Pluto Press.

Oosterman, M., Schuengel, C., Slot, N. W., Bullens, R. A. R., & Doreleijers, T. A. H. (2006). Disruptions in foster care: A review and meta-analysis. *Children and Youth Services Review, 29*(1), 53–76.

Prevatt-Goldstein, B. (1999). Direct work with Black children with one White parent. In R. Barn (Ed.), *Working with Black children and adolescents in need.* London: BAAF.

Ritchie, C. (2005). Looked after children: Time for change? *British Journal of Social Work, 35*(5), 761–767.

Small, J. (1986). Transracial placement: Conflict and contradiction. In S. Ahmed, J. Cheetham, & J. Small (Eds.), *Social work with Black children and their families*. London: BAAF.

Song, M. (2003). *Choosing ethnic identity*. Cambridge: Polity Press.

Stein, M. (1999). Leaving care: Reflections and challenges. In O. Stevenson (Ed.), *Child welfare in the UK*. Oxford: Blackwell.

Thoburn, J. (2005). Permanent family placement for children of dual heritage: Issues arising from a longitudinal study. In T. Okitikpi (Ed.), *Working with children of mixed parentage*. Dorset: Russell House.

Thoburn, J., Norford, L., & Rashid, S. P. (2000a). *Permanent family placement for children of minority ethnic origin*. London: Jessica Kingsley.

Thoburn, J., Wilding, J., & Watson, J. (2000b). *Family support in cases of emotional abuse and neglect*. London: The Stationery Office.

Tizard, B., & Phoenix, A. (1993). *Black, White or mixed race?: Race and racism in the lives of young people of mixed parentage*. London: Routledge.

Wilson, A. (1987). *Mixed race children: A study of identity*. London: Allen and Unwin.

Wright Mills, C. (1959). *The sociological imagination*. New York: Oxford University Press.

Websites

Care Leavers Transition to Adulthood. (2015). https://www.nao.org.uk/report/care-leavers-transitions-to-adulthood/ (accessed on 12 November 2015).

Collier, F. (2010). https://www.thefosteringnetwork.org.uk/sites/www.fostering.net/files/content/cofc-report.pdf (accessed on 12 May 2010).

Hughes, B. (2008). www.ofstednews.ofsted.gov.uk/article/213 (accessed on 11 November 2008).

Peters, F. V. (2010). *Who cares about mixed race: Experiences of young people in an inner city Borough* (unpublished thesis). http://research.gold.ac.uk/2885/1/SOC_thesis_Peters_2010.pdf

Visual Media

Dispatches. (2010). Undercover social worker. Episode aired 7 June 2010, directed by Mathieson, M.

3

Understanding Mixedness: Concepts, Categories, and People

In the recent past, US groups clamoured for official recognition of the inclusion of multiracial and biracial classifications. Identity groups were consulted in order to glean information on the categories in current use (Aspinall 2009: 57). In 2001 US Census adopted a multi-ticking system for respondents to tick all that apply to their heritage (2001) using the language of race: biracial and multiracial (Hispanic and Latino being the only ethnic categories). The US Census was defined by the Office of Management and Budget (OMB) and the United States Census Bureau and showed an increase in citizens choosing a biracial or multiracial identity, demonstrating fluidity and a blurring of racial boundaries (Bratter 2007).

However, the Census categories are now considered problematic as they can reinforce racial hierarchies (Spencer 2006) by positioning mixed people in a buffer group between black and white, which has led to a number of objections to the biracial and multiracial category. Notably, mixed people are leaving the black category for a more favoured status, resulting in what Gallagher (2004) calls 'redistricting', resulting in much smaller numbers of African Americans appearing in official population counts. Civil rights leaders oppose the multiracial box as it makes it harder to measure discrimination and has been said to endanger affirmative

© The Editor(s) (if applicable) and The Author(s) 2016   **23**
F. Peters, *Fostering Mixed Race Children*,
DOI 10.1057/978-1-137-54184-0_3

action (Song 2010). Racial and ethnic groups have a real and vested interest in identity, and identification is a strategy in gaining consensus and belonging. Identity is both active and performed in order to be recognized and socially legitimated. As Bauman (1996: 19) states, 'One thinks of identity whenever one is not sure how to place oneself among the evident variety of behavioural styles and patterns, and how to make sure the people around would accept this placement as right and proper … Identity is the name given to escape from that uncertainty'.

The development of the mixed ethnic classification in the UK Census for England and Wales emerged through the recognition of high rates of interethnic and interracial relationships among specific groups, and multiple allegiances were noted during the 1990s (McKenney and Bennett 1994). Over several decades increased interest in the identity choices of mixed people was in part due to the strong population growth shown in the 2001 Census for England and Wales (Song 2003). Census agencies in England and Wales devise categories, which they then test on the general public to gain consensus. The categories are then adopted by government for all data collection, creating a single source of ethnic and racial vocabulary. How the categories are decided has implications for not only how people see themselves but also for how legitimate their identifications are, as we cannot use labels that do not exist. The Office for National Statistics (ONS) remains responsive to the development of adequate classifications in the Census for England and Wales, deciding on categories and subsequently testing them on the general public for popular endorsement. Although categories close down options of description, the free text box offers a space to write in a specific heritage which more accurately describes one's identification.

Despite the inclusion of mixed as an ethnic classification in the UK Census in 2001, its underpinnings as a social category constitutive of a group remain ambiguous. The mixed classification is an important aspect of social legitimacy and recognition; however, defining the parameters of the mixed category along the racial and ethnic boundaries that constitute it often conceals its internal diversity (Ali 2003; Aspinall and Song 2013; Caballero et al. 2008; Song 2003; Tizard and Phoenix 1993). Although ethnic monitoring and classification is an important tool in the recognition of mixed people, it remains to be seen how the information will be used.[1] In the 2011 Census for England and Wales, under the heading 'Mixed/Multiple ethnic groups', respondents were offered a pan-ethnic classification within which four 'mixed' options were presented: 'White and Black Caribbean', 'White and Black African', 'White and Asian', and 'Any other mixed background'. What we now know from this data gathering is that approximately 677,000 (1.2 % of population) people in Britain described themselves as mixed in the 2001 Census for England and Wales, of whom 360,355 or 45 % were under the age of sixteen years while only 19 % of the general population were under sixteen. Children are more likely to have their identity ascribed by their parents on the Census form, and this may be inconsistent over time as identity changes during adolescence. According to the Census, 80 % of mixed people were born in Britain. Ninety per cent of mixed respondents described their national identity as British (ONS 2001). The high percentage of mixed respondents claiming a British heritage illustrates that identity and belonging do not hold nationality and ethnicity as incompatible. Mixed people tend to be concentrated in urban areas and in some of the most deprived parts of the country. The population of the mixed category almost doubled in the decade between 2001 and 2011. By 2011, the England and Wales Census recorded 1,224,400 (2.2 % of the population) as mixed, of whom 603,398 were under sixteen years. This young age structure and the rapidly increasing mixed population presents future challenges for developing Census categories, as one-fifth of young people report three or more groups in their heritage (Aspinall and Song 2013).

Future categories need further differentiation to include those with multiple mixtures, and how this population might be asked to classify is a topic for discussion in the ONS's 2021 Census Development Programme. Specifying all ethnic heritages or ticking all boxes that apply will capture patterns and trends of mixing as well as population count but may make categorization untenable.

The future development of the Census is likely to encourage people to state their preferred identity as opposed to any direct operational heritage

---

[1] There are issues surrounding the durability of the classification that invites respondents to state ethnic heritage. See Owen (2001) for further discussion.

or ancestry. Aspinall states: '[t]here is little room in the Census for operational questions about origins due to the ONS's insistence on capturing how people think about their identity', and confirms that '[i]dentity is on the ascendancy in government discourse on diversity' (Aspinall 2009: 67). In relation to reliability a 'tick all that apply' approach is more consistent (64). However, the research project tested this option, and respondents did not understand the method, resulting in poor data quality. During the next ten years, it is likely that multi-ticking across boxes will become preferable, allowing people to select as many heritages as they feel reflect their identity, but currently the public is unfamiliar with this approach.

The mixed category does have some conceptual issues such as being reductionist, concealing heterogeneity within the Asian classification, not addressing respondents who change their identity over time, and sustaining colour-based ethnic groups. It is important to pay attention to the ethnic combinations and trends of mixing that denote other socio-economic factors that lead to inequalities within local populations. Public policy informed by research that captures the complexity and variability among individuals must guard against making assumptions about such a diverse mixed group (Aspinall and Song 2013).

Data Collection for Children Looked After and Their Families

The Department of Education statistical collection return SSDA903 provides guidelines to clarify how practitioners ought to collect information on children looked after in their local authority during 2016–2017 (see Appendix). 'Children are asked which code best describes their origin. If this is not possible, the authority should code the child in accordance with their own observations' (DfE 2015: 35), affirming the ultimate reliance and influence of colour-coded ethnic categories of belonging based upon visual appearance and the biological persistence of race-making. The code set for ethnic origin within the mixed classification now mirrors the Census categories, and all begin with a white classification. The category which was previously black Caribbean and white has now become 'Black Caribbean and White'. Significantly, only the white category is offered a British nationality despite the 90 % of mixed respondents who identified as British in the 2011 Census. The shift in prefacing mixed with the white category may have implications at a local level, ultimately impacting how mixed children are understood and placed in families (Fig. 3.1).

Coding children according to ethnic origin is 'not an exact science' but one that depends on local practice and what the child and parents perceive themselves to be (DfE 2015). In order to assist coders, there is also a table for 'country of origin', which comprises mainly countries currently experiencing migration to England. If a child and parents are uncertain of which ethnic code applies to their country of origin, the additional table enables the practitioners to code according to their own 'observations' (skin colour) using their discretion (2015). There is no code for children of unknown origin, and in these cases the practitioner would use local knowledge, observations at interviews, and informed guesses to arrive at an adequate category.

Local authorities that do undertake ethnic monitoring of children and young people in residential and foster care do not always accurately

WBRI	White British
WIRI	White Irish
WOTH	Any other White background
WIRT	Traveller of Irish heritage
WROM	Gypsy/Roma
MWBC	White and Black Caribbean
MWBA	White and Black African
MWBA	White and Black Asian
MOTH	Any other Mixed
AIND	Indian
APKN	Pakistani
ABAN	Bangladeshi
AOTH	Any Other Asian
BCRB	Black Caribbean
BAFR	Black African
BOTH	Any Other Black
CHNE	Chinese
OOTH	Any Other Ethnic Group
REFU	Refused
NOBT	Information not yet obtained

Fig. 3.1 Code set for ethnic origin local authority guidance

Details provided in 2014 Statistical First Release	Proposed new details for 2015
Ethnic origin	Ethnic origin
White	White
White British	Mixed
White Irish	Asian or Asian British
Traveller of Irish Heritage	Black or Black British
Gypsy/Roma	Other ethnic groups
Any other White background	Other
Mixed	
White and Black Caribbean	
White and Black African	
White and Asian	
Any other mixed background	
Asian or Asian British	
Indian	
Pakistani	
Bangladeshi	
Any other Asian background	
Black or Black British	
Caribbean	
African	
Any other Black background	
Other ethnic groups	
Chinese	
Any other ethnic group	
Other	
Refused	
Information not yet available	

Fig. 3.2 All children looked after at 31 March by gender, age at 31 March, category of need, and ethnic origin

or consistently record ethnic and racial heritage (Barn 1993). Due to these inconsistencies, the number of mixed children looked after is subject to fluctuations of approximately 10 %.[2] The figures vary at the local authority level as more economically deprived areas have higher numbers of children looked after. Local authority statistics are reliant on categorizations in use by the Census, but these classifications lead to a narrow assignment of heritage and are unable to include multiple ethnic heritages of children who have two mixed race parents or who have a mix of black, minority, and ethnic heritage, for example, Asian and African.

The Department for Education's Children and Early Years Data Unit is proposing changes to the way that data on all children looked after in England are published as part of the Statistical First Release. CoramBAAF developed a table to show how these proposed changes

---

[2] Ethnic monitoring across social services departments is inconsistent, patchy, and often results in inaccurate recordings of ethnicity. This can be due to unknown paternity. Visual appearance can also influence how classification is recorded.

in relation to ethnicity would be presented (see Fig. 3.2). Notably, there would not be any published information on the ethnic heritage of mixed children looked after, meaning that children with mixtures of white, Caribbean, African, and Asian heritage will be collated together into a single group. CoramBAAF has stated [e]thnic data is required to understand differences between rates of entry, length of stay and rates of leaving care for different ethnic groups and to avoid exclusions of groups of children and inform future resources and service planning. Ethnicity is a crucial aspect of identity and often a determining factor in care planning (specifically for mixed race children of white and black Caribbean heritage) and underpins whether they become looked after or not. Maintaining ethnic data is vital for measuring any over-representation of disadvantaged groups and addressing subsequent need. Ultimately, accurate coding of ethnicity relies on practitioners making a comprehensive and accurate assessment of the needs of the child and allocating resources to support necessary cultural, linguistic, or religious provision.

The Prospective Foster Carer Report (Form F) is used to gather information from prospective adopters and foster families. Developed by the British Association for Adoption and Fostering (BAAF) it is seen as a consistent way to measure an applicant's suitability for fostering or adoption and is a robust and consistent matching tool. Section A on the form examines the respondent's ethnicity within a framework endorsed by the Equality and Human Rights Commission. One aspect of the assessment is for applicants to develop a family tree or equivalent structure, outlining transitions and events that have had a lasting impact into adulthood. Prospective carer's identity development is explored for signs of healthy self-esteem and how they might relate to the needs of a child from a diverse background. Community, family, and social links are explored to discover whether they may have any negative attitudes. During the course of six to twelve visits, a final portfolio of the applicants' lives is created. The portfolio is used to determine their suitability for fostering or adoption and, if successful, informs their matching profile.

Mixed Classifications and Residential Care

The growing attention to mixed race children in care is partly due to their enduring presence coupled with the official emergence of the mixed classification in data collection. In relation to ethnic background of children looked after, 75% of all children are white, children of mixed ethnicity are the largest ethnic group looked after in England at 9%, black children are at 7%, Asian at 4%, and any other at 3% (DfE, 2016). Conversely, in the US context, data collection states that 9% of children in care are multiracial and a distinction is made as to what comprises that classification: American Indian, Alaskan Native, Asian, Native Hawaiian, Other Pacific Islander, or two more races (Aspinall and Song, 2013).

The experiences of mixed children in the care system have been a long-standing concern and constitute a serious social problem as the population increases. Their care needs are recognized as different to those of black or white children (Barn and Harman 2006; Okitikpi 2005; Owusu-Bempah 2005). A series of reviews and studies indicate that mixed children 'present a dilemma for social workers' in terms of appropriate placements (Barn 1999: 281), and they 'continue to be disadvantaged in the system' (ibid.: 34). A longitudinal study showed that 18% of 'mixed race heritage children were able to retain contact with a birth parent or be placed with a sibling' in contrast to 38% of young people with two same race parents (Thoburn 2005: 118). The findings also suggest that mixed race heritage children wait longer in unstable or short-term care and that 84% are placed with white families, compared to 55% of those with two black parents from the same background (ibid.: 117). These statistics suggest it is 'possible that these decisions were made on shades of colour rather than actual needs and concerns' (ibid.: 61). Research based in thirteen local authorities in England undertook quantitative evaluation of the notes made by social workers about children being admitted into care (Bebbington and Miles 1989). The findings suggest that the classification of mixed race could be considered an indicator of disadvantage, alongside poverty, poor health, and poor housing. They also suggest that all other factors being equal, such as living conditions and family type, mixed race children and young people are still two and a half times more likely than white children to be taken into care. As Morley and Street (2014: 6) suggest, 'Although there are large numbers of policy documents focusing on race and equality aspects of assessment and service delivery, very little attention is currently paid to mixed race as a possible additional factor to be taken into account in assessment and intervention'.

Abuse or neglect is the most cited reason for the admission of mixed children and young people into care: for mixed white and black Caribbean children and young people it is cited in 62 % of cases and for mixed white and black African children and young people it is cited in 60 %. These figures are in line with the national average of 60 % for this category of need (Owen and Statham 2009). Acute distress in families is the second most cited reason for admission of mixed white and black Caribbean children and young people. The figures show that 'acute distress' accounts for just over 9 % of admissions to care and that for mixed white and black African children and young people it is also 9 % (ibid). These figures are in line with the national average across all ethnic groups at just over 10 % (ibid). The data held on children's admission to care is categorized according to the main reason for admission while contributing family circumstances remain unknown (Barn 1993, 1999; Bebbington and Miles 2003). Mixed race children are over-represented in every category of need in Children's Social Care, comprising 5 % of all children in need (double their percentage of the general population); over 7 % on the Child Protection Register, and almost 8 % on the Looked After Children Register (Owen and Statham 2009).

Looked-after children with a mixed classification are a broad and diverse group with varying placement needs, yet assumptions about how they ought to be socialized (into an appropriate identity) often rely on racialized positions of practitioners and cultural, localized practices in Children's Social Care departments. Race mixing is continually evolving to encompass new migration and multiple heritages, and Children's Social Care reflects these new trends in its decision-making processes by integrating the changing patterns of ethnic and racial mixing in the local population. Training practitioners need to consider the impact of a mixed classification in more detail beyond the level of identity, and engaging in open discussion about the inherent diversity of mixedness can shift thinking and possibly change outcomes for children in care. Importantly, mixed children in care are a rich and important source of opinions and feelings and offer a wealth of lived experience to share with practitioners in enabling greater understanding (Peters 2010).

Social Legitimacy of Mixed Families and Race Mixing

The beginning of significant attention to race mixing came during the 1940s at the cusp of post-war immigration to Britain from the Commonwealth. The growth of the half-caste (primarily children of migrant fathers and white British mothers) population became subject to welfare discourses and interventions into communities in English cities. The Home Office proposed that one possible solution to this problem was to ship the babies of unions between working-class white women and black seafaring and army men to America to be adopted and raised in black families. The black British population opposed this (Solomos and Back 1996: 180). Yet political policy and welfare concerns from the post-war era to today have consistently debated the question of what to do with the children of inter-racial relationships. The value of the brown baby as a symbol of racial harmony bears no relation to the statistics, which present the mixed children of a white mother and a black father as most likely to enter care under the age of one year (Selwyn 2008). In the popular comedy sketch show, *Harry Enfield and Chums* (1994), a working-class white woman, Waynetta Slob, expresses her desire for a brown baby. This comedy sketch highlights the assumptions about mixed families and their position as part of a wider popular narrative of undesirable race mixing taking place between lower-class white women and hypersexual black men (Caballero 2008). Understandings of race through mixing and mixedness have been shaped by social, political, and legal discourse, and these have had consequences for how mixed families have been understood in wider social life and in Children's Social Care. It is acknowledged that '[m]ixed race relationships per se put extra strain on the family' (Morley and Street 2014: 67).

The attitude of social workers who are unable to think about mixed relationships in positive ways has also been cited as a factor in the increased admissions of mixed children into care, particularly those from white, lone mother families (Banks 1995). Research findings suggest that mixed children and young people with lone white mothers were taken into care in 59 % of referrals. White children and young people with lone white mothers were taken into care in only 49 % of all referrals (Barn 1999). Judgements about the 'ability of lone white mothers being unable to care for mixed children' have been cited as responsible for their high care admission rates (Barn 1993; Katz 1996). Accusations surrounding the cultural competency of lone white mothers are asserted in relation to their inability to socialize mixed children with regard to culture, deal with racism or racial abuse, manage hair and skin care, and provide culturally appropriate food. As Olumide states, these '[p]rocesses of racialization and race thinking allow issues of entitlement to arise around the mother's right to raise her child' (Olumide 2002: 131).

Further, the link between lone motherhood and poverty is established through 'lone mothers' vulnerability to poverty, not lone motherhood itself' (Gillies 2007: 19). Lone mothers are more likely to experience difficulty with childcare when employed in poorly paid positions or only working during term time with reduced school hours. Long-term poverty is often a characteristic of lone parents, unemployed parents, teenage parents, families with children under five, and families with a large number of children (Gillies 11). Further longitudinal research by Dearing and colleagues (2004) concluded that mothers affected by poverty are more likely to become depressed, which is likely to adversely affect the quality of parenting. Poverty is most usefully understood to be relative and can be described as 'Individuals, families and groups in the population … [who] lack the resources to obtain the types of diet, participate in the activities and have the living conditions and amenities which are customary, or at least widely encouraged or approved in the societies to which they belong' (Townsend 1979: 31).

An analysis of the relationship between social class and depression suggests mothers from a lower social class are more prone to depression: 39 % versus 6 % of mothers from higher social classes (Brown and Harris 1978).[3]

---

[3] Although it could be argued that mothers who are depressed and living in poverty are also more likely to be unemployed and the inverse could be considered a possibility.

Depressed parents living in impoverished conditions are more likely to become stressed, angry, or irritable, and this affects parenting style. 'Parenting style and not poverty per se, affects children's outcomes in negative ways' (Katz et al. 2007: 18). Further, economically deprived parents from different ethnic groups respond differently to the stresses of poverty (Barnes 2004a, b; Marsh and Mackay 1994). Research findings show a correlation between poverty as a cause of stress and poverty as a cause of child abuse and neglect (Briggs and Hawkins 1996; Katz et al. 2007; Pelton 2015). Despite high levels of abuse and neglect in all groups, white and mixed ethnicity children were more likely to be referred for neglect (Selwyn et al. 2008).

The National Society for the Prevention of Cruelty to Children (NSPCC) estimates that one in five children is exposed to domestic violence (NSPCC 2015). Links between domestic violence and child abuse show that between 30 % and 60 % of all child abuse cases also involve domestic violence in the home (Hester et al. 2000; Radford and Hester 2006). Masson and colleagues (2008) investigated 400 files of children involved in care proceedings, and domestic violence was recorded in over half the files. The leading charity Women's Aid cites that 'Two women each week are killed by violence in the home accounting for forty percent of all murders; sixty eight percent of women experience post-traumatic stress disorder; forty eight percent have depression and eighteen percent attempt to commit suicide' (Womens Aid 2008). The Adoption and Children Act 2002 in England and Wales amended the definition of significant harm provided by the Children Act 1989, adding a new category of 'impairment suffered from hearing or seeing the ill-treatment of another'; consequently being a witness to violence in the home often leads to child removal. In addition to the power dynamic of gender is class stratification, and it is the poor and the disenfranchised who are the most likely to experience removal of their children to a better cultural, material, or spiritual experience. 'The operation of care cannot be separated from the exercise of power. To separate children from families, sending them away to regulate them makes the care system a political site where the exercise and distribution of power is contested' (Frost et al. 1999: 25).

Understanding the Mixed Family

The Labour Force Survey shows that 50 % of Caribbean men and 33 % of Caribbean women are in a relationship with someone of another ethnic group. There are more children under the age of fifteen years with one black and one white parent than there are with two black parents (Owen 2007). There are indications that mixed families outside of contact with social services are predominately middle-class, highly educated, and living in some of the most affluent areas in Britain (Caballero et al. 2008). Two-parent families comprise 87 % of mixed racial and ethnic households with dependent children, whereas the national average is only 65 % (ibid.: 14).

The family can be understood as the site of social reproduction through processes of socialization disseminated through parenting (Knowles 1996). Understanding families in relation to each other and in relation to society is usually accomplished through attention to behaviours seen as acceptable or unacceptable. Families who experience intervention are notably those who exhibit behaviours on the margins of acceptability in relation to child welfare, and they become subject to scrutiny from professionals (Gillies 2007). Knowles argues that through these discourses and narratives of family life, meaning is generated about what constitutes the family (1996: 30). Mixed families can be understood through attention to how power circulates inside the family in sexualized and gendered relationships and through the understandings of the family from other family members and outsiders (Alibhai-Brown 2001).

Race mixing is considered outside notions of normative heterosexual relationships. Butler (1993: 167) states that racial mixing and homosexuality 'both converge at and as the constitutive outside', being outside of dominant underpinnings of (hetero)sexuality and race. Sexual relationships between populations from white Europe and black Africa, Asia, and the Caribbean are unions that provoke strong emotions (Alibhai-Brown 2001; Olumide 2002). Katz (1996) asks why people from different racial groups form liaisons which produce children of mixed parentage, given the antagonism between the races. What are the interpersonal dynamics in such relationships? The context of the relationships, the dynamics of the interracial couple/family, and social ambivalence towards such relationships are crucial aspects of understanding mixing and mixedness and possibly the consequences of mixed children's enduring relationship to care. These debates are considered by Barn (1993, 1999), Barn and Harman (2005), Olumide (2002), and Okitikpi (2005).

Okitikpi (2005) points towards a list of seven motivating factors that enable social work practitioners to make sense of mixed relationships. These suppositions range between racial hatred/denial (Fanon 1952), social mobility and cultural inclusion (Wade 1993), economic mobility (Ferguson 1982), sexual and colour curiosity (Gill 1995), revenge for racial oppression (Cleaver 1968), shortage of same race partners (Kannan 1973), and mutual affection and shared interests (Duck 1993). 'These assertions often provide the backdrop against which attitudes towards and approaches to working with mixed race children and their families are developed by welfare professionals' (Okitikpi 2005: 5). Mixed families are therefore positioned as difficult to understand within welfare intervention, and thus interactions are guided by assumptions that such couples could not share the same levels of love that mono-cultural couples might (2005).

A Foucauldian framework helps to situate how the mixed family is constituted within specific social productions across time and space (Foucault 1977: 102). Firstly, the mixed family is constituted in relation to the power to name it, study it, and intervene in it. These interventions are aimed at controlling both the reproduction of the mixed family and the appropriate cultural socialization of children within it. Secondly, mixed families are constituted through enduring relationships in which power is invested in specific positions such as mother, father, and child. Such positions can be attached to roles and narratives in which men are seen as violent, women as passive, and children as victims. Further, the roles within the family—the lone white mother, absent black father, and mixed up child—are constituted by discourses aimed at their regulation and organized through paradigms of race and ethnicity. Thirdly, families are 'disciplined, regulated and organised' (Foucault 209) through techniques of surveillance, assessment, and correction. These techniques are used within the family through traditions, behaviours, and responsibilities given through power invested in specific roles and also outside of the family in more formal structures such as schools, hospitals, social welfare agencies, and the law. Familial power thus works to name, to position and subject, and to govern. Mixed families in both social work and wider socio-political discourse are considered 'essentially unacceptable' (Okitikpi 2005) and have been subjected to discursive practices aimed at both regulating reproduction and controlling the socialization of mixed children, leading to consistently high instances of child removal from mixed families across the globe (Olumide 2002).

Olumide (2002) states that in societies structured by white supremacy and racial difference, the removal of mixed children from families illustrates how power and status have been contested across the boundaries of race. French Indochina and Australia implemented the separation of families through notions of racial difference (ibid.: 80). Economic resources in Australia were made available for the surveillance and correction of mixed families for appropriate cultural socialization (Stoler 1995). As Olumide's (2002) historical excavation of socio-political attitudes to mixing and mixedness shows, nations have been built upon the eradication or the cultural assimilation of mixed people, and such practices have been instrumental in nation-building through policing the borders towards the eradication or control of difference. Direct policies concerned with the regulation and control of race mixing impact the perception of mixed families. Olumide (2002: 83) argues: '[p]resent-day discourses of "cultural heritage" carry in similar ways intimations of race thinking'. Intervention aimed to correct mixed families is only ever aimed at families who are poor or powerless, and therefore mixedness and mixing operate through race and/or culture and shift according to other variables of difference—primarily poverty.

Research by Caballero (2008) on mixed families shows they have a middle-class dimension and that over half the children have married or cohabiting parents, overturning the image of race mixing being an inner city phenomenon characterized by subsequent lone parenting. Mixed families feel their race, ethnicity, culture, and religion are just another part of their lives (Caballero 2008). Social class impacts whether families share parenting practices, for example, two families, one working class and the other middle class, both white English and Jamaican, are 'not guaranteed to share approaches and experiences' (ibid.: 3).

Feminist analyses of the family, and in particular mothering, have neglected research on mixed families (Olumide 2002; Twine 1999a, b).

Sociological analysis of the mixed family remains within the confines of the socialization of mixed children (Caballero et al. 2008; Wilson 1987), making the family a site solely for social and cultural reproduction. Mixed families have been studied in relation to care admissions, making the lone white mother the subject of research (Barn 1999; Barn and Harman 2005).[4] Attention is paid to the experiences of white women in mixed relationships (Alibhai-Brown 2001; Barn and Harman 2006; Mckenzie 2009; Olumide 2002). It is argued that their social isolation and lack of support is said to be a factor in the high care admissions of mixed children (Barn and Harman 2006). Alibhai-Brown (2001) suggests that dealing with racism for the first time, as a white woman within a mixed relationship or as a mother of a mixed child without coping strategies or support, can be difficult. Such incidents of racism against white women can lead to what Olumide names as attacks on the 'social legitimacy' of the mixed family whereby mixed couples are seen as not belonging together—the seemingly irreconcilable and visible difference of race (Olumide 2002: 108).

Olumide states: '[a]t the point of its perceived mixture, whiteness becomes overtly racialized and gendered. It seems reasonable to pay attention to the career of whiteness as it moves between its "pure" (and often undifferentiated) states, into areas of its mixture where it becomes a compromised privilege' (2002: 31).

Mckenzie's (2009) research on the St. Ann's estate in Nottingham offers insights into the coping strategies claimed by working-class white women in mixed families whose successful parenting is dependent on finding value in Jamaican cultural forms and moving away from normative white working-class culture. The strategies used by the women on the St. Ann's estate contribute to the successful parenting of mixed children within the types of families who may usually be targets for welfare intervention. Doreen Massey (1994) claims that all social identities, social categories, and hierarchies articulate in some way with place and are routed through discourses such as race, gender, and class. Concurring, Jacqueline Nassy Brown (2005: 242) further suggests that

---

[4] Little attention has been paid to the absent black father; his naming as absent from family life has already been constructed and critiqued within models of matriarchal family structures.

place, local and global are not abstract, objective, neutral spatial constructs. Rather, the particular ways in which they get invoked and naturalized—both textually and in actual social life—are directly implicated in the subject positions we know as gender, race, and nation.

The dis-identification (Skeggs 1997) of white mothers from normative white working-class values informs a shift in their parenting, through cultural practices that offer alternative value to their marginalized experiences.

Many geographical locations within the Western or European city are characterized by hybrid and multiple identities or 'superdiversity' (Vertovec 2007) and are seen as preferable locations for raising families, confirming them as places where race mixing is more prevalent. Thoburn and colleagues' (2000a, b) research also notes the importance of geographical location for the success of long-term fostering with white carers, and the location of carers in multiethnic areas is a theme that arises in other research findings (Barn et al. 2005; Fatimilehin 2005; Robinson 2000; Tizard and Phoenix 1993). Children and young people who grow up in residential homes with a multiracial staff and in multiethnic areas are said to receive good, positive, and appropriate racial and ethnic socialization, leading to an awareness of self and ethnic group belonging as well as awareness of strategies to cope with race discrimination (Barn 2011). Such locations are seen to offer an everyday, lived experience where mixed families are seen as ordinary, playing a part in how young people establish a sense of self through family structure, friendship groups, and the visible difference among a multiethnic population within their interactions (Caballero et al. 2008).

Experiences of Racialization

The language to describe mixed people is a source of tension as the evolution of the term is entangled in discussions about the usefulness of race and in debates about racialization as a pseudoscientific construct and its subsequent reification through discourse. Class stratification and geographical location also determine which terms of description are applicable. It is often asserted that the middle classes prefer to use the term 'mixed race' while the working classes sometimes use 'half-caste' (Ali 2003; Dewan 2008; Tizard and Phoenix 1993). There is evidence that among young people the term 'half-caste' is being re-claimed and used without its negative connotations (Lincoln 2008). Social work practitioners and policy makers are divided in how they classify and label mixed people and are caught in the tension between whether to continue to classify mixed race as black (Banks 1995; Maximé 1993), black with a white parent (Prevatt-Goldstein 1999), black but of mixed parentage, or mixed. There is further debate over 'mixed race, mixed parentage, mixed origin, dual heritage, or multiple heritage' (Barn and Harman 2006: 1310). It is suggested that the multiple terms in use signal a group in the making and not a fixed group (DaCosta 2009). It is clear that the terminology of mixed remains unsettled and contested, and mixed young people in foster care are caught within a complex political dilemma over racial and ethnic classification and subsequent description.

This book uses the terms 'mixed race' and 'mixed' to describe people of black African or Caribbean and white British parentage, since these terms are most favoured by the participants and are thus legitimate as a form of description. I also use the term 'race', as it remains a material force in how people who are subject to racialization are able to live. Research shows that mixed people with black heritage still have limited ethnic options as they are more routinely placed into the black category (Aspinall and Song 2013). Further, those of mixed black and white heritage note the significance of colour and the negative racialization of black people in institutions and public settings (184). Mixed race acknowledges signs of visible racial mixing which structure experience through processes of racialization, which in the site of Children's Social Care leads to adverse experiences.

Examining mixedness, as a classification and category through the experiential, finds similarity across race, ethnicity, and religion, rendering these variables a specific point of investigation as they intersect with gender, class, culture, or age. This intersection is the lived experience, which is acted upon by others and allows for an unpacking of the processes of racialization in the site of foster care through the everyday experiences of young people. Race is only one aspect of identity, but one that can override other identifications such as class, sex, and gender (Mama 1995).

Race-making is a social practice made through processes of racialization that emerge within populations in which 'race is used to categorise individuals or behaviour' (Miles 1989: 73). Race is made among people to assign identities to others that somehow characterize them through a bodily schema and in this way racial identities become fixed and unchanging.

Race is made by people in and through social practices and is implicit in the way that social meaning is constructed (Knowles 2003). Deconstruction is useful for the purpose of understanding race-making processes within specific sites and contexts. 'If we move race from the agenda, we cannot at the same time claim that race prejudice, social ascription, marginalisation and discrimination exist, and challenge such inequalities in society' (Dewan 2008: 9). Investigating the experiences of mixed people does not suggest that race exists as a discrete entity but that it is actively made by people and has social consequences for the lived experiences of those who are subject to racialization practices. As Robinson (2005: 77) asserts, '[r]acial identity does not imply acceptance of race as real, but acknowledges the social and political reality that people live in societies in which race identities are attributed to them ... and these have real consequences for their experiences of life'. Race leaves no enduring identity among people and is not characterized by universal features of human existence, but race does have consequences for lives.

In the USA the rule of hypo-descent designated all mixed people as black in order to withhold the economic legacies of slave owners' profits from their mulatto offspring. In 1705 the state of Virginia passed a law which classified the child according to fractional inheritance of blood ranging from mulatto to octoroon. Virginia officials declared that all those with one drop of black blood must be considered black and the bondage of 'Blackness' was defined and made universal through legislation and its associated practices. The aim of such a system was to obliterate the status and resources attached to the economic, cultural, and political value of white heritage among the growing population of mixed people. Their white heritage was erased by the practices of legislation which endeavoured to 'deny them inheritance and privileges based on their white origins' (Owusu-Bempah 2005: 28).

These ghostly patterns are discernible in current thinking about the role of the biological in ascertaining belonging. For example, Children's

Social Care utilizes DNA testing to determine the ethnic heritage of mixed children with unknown paternity (reinstating the underpinnings of the one-drop law). These current practices of defining black heritage and ancestry are then used to determine what type of racial and ethnic heritage is most desirable for planning a future foster or adoptive family. Young people, when aiming to describe how they understand and think about their identification, use fractional and splitting approaches to describe, in a more nuanced way, their heritage. Race is a political category used to determine experience and opportunity and has roots in historical transatlantic practices—in the site of British Children's Social Care in England, racial classification is the determining factor for underpinning placement-matching guidelines. Olumide (2002) confirms that processes of racialization construct the mixed race condition and that mixed people become subjects situated within discursive repertoires of race and race-making. Hence, the emphasis on how the site of Children's Social Care shapes and situates specific experiences of children and young people in foster care.

Visible differences such as skin colour become signifiers of unseen qualities, such as morality, sexuality, or some inner schema of inheritance believed to be embedded in DNA. (Such an understanding informs how race mixing is understood as an irreconcilable difference.) These signifiers are relational and linked to variables such as gender, sexuality, location, and class. Hence, race can never be the same across all sites; such sliding signifiers cannot be fixed or certain, nor can they assign specific characteristics (Cohen 1994). The complexity of defining mixedness entails the recognition of race as a sliding signifier (Fanon 1968) that constructs racially or ethnically distinct categories. Sliding referents work to re-position race (mixedness) according to the logic of the site (Children's Social Care) and the actions and identifications of those within it—parents, practitioners, and children. These categories are always subject to individual understandings, environmental influence, and the social position or status of people in that site. Hence, there is a widespread acceptance and recognition of race as fluid, multiple, and under the influence of the environment, which determines how we underpin and act upon race (Butler 1993). Mixed, as a classification, demonstrates that even despite its ambiguous boundaries of belonging, the disruption and the deconstruction of the existing socio-political bi-racial landscape is taking place. Current tension around race rests upon a move towards relegating race as a phenomenon that affects life chances, in balance with the recognition that racial mixing is creating social, cultural, and political dimensions that destabilize the idea of separate and distinct groups known solely through ancestry, customs, and an awareness of belonging. As Appiah (2000: 33) clarifies, '[understanding the idea of race involves grasping how people think about races: what they take to be the central truth about races; under what sort of circumstances they will apply the idea of race; what consequences of action will flow from that application'.

Race is a factor in all of our lives. No one is untouched by it. For some it may be invasive. For others it operates at the periphery of their lives. Race structures the world we live in, how we live in it, and how we engage with the environment around us. Race evolves over time and across geographical locations to change its parameters of belonging and has no intrinsic value as it shifts according to time and space. The enduring presence of skin colour and (mis)recognition reifies race by fixing the visual markers of race on the body. These markers are subject to individual and societal readings that shift through contexts. Race appears as an intellectual mythical exercise yet has real socio-economic manifestations and political consequences. Holt (2002) argues that the very nature of race is ambiguous and chameleon-like, and thus its temporal and spatial resilience is its key feature. The consequence of this is that any attempt to harness the way that race works, or contain its key manifestations, is likely to be anachronistic. Race is a reality in the way that people organize their lives individually and collectively as families and social groups. Even though race has a historical trajectory, it is a 'complex, lived, material reality' (Frankenberg 1997: 22). Race confers a more complex social reality due to its structuring presence within social institutions, which operate through hierarchies of difference. In the setting of Children's Social Care, race is an enduring category, which over the years has led to consistently adverse consequences for racialized groups of people.

Attempts to theorize the lived experience of mixed people therefore rely on the 'idea that personhood is socially constructed' (Dewan 2008: 35).

Implicit in the idea of personhood is the understanding that we are social beings who form ourselves within social relationships (Ifekwunigwe 1999; Mahtani 2005; Parker and Song 2001; Rockquemore and Brunsma 2002; Root 2006). An examination of mixedness requires engagement with debates about individual identities and about who is and who is not mixed in the context of how social life is organized. It is also about how these boundaries of ethnic difference and racial sameness can be mobilized in non-exclusionary ways (Ali 2003). However, such an engagement also speaks to discourses which have placed mixed people as black, marginal, or confused (Ifekwunigwe 1999; Root 1996). Mixedness has been seen as a truly post-modern identity for being able to bring together different cultures (Mahtani 2005). In this way mixed people are seen as race pedagogues (Camper 2004), which 'leaves the race work up to mixed people' (ibid.: 181). The multiple affiliations of mixedness make it difficult to define as a category (Ali 2003), and, further, not all individuals experience mixedness in the same way (Dewan 2008).

The development of mixedness beyond individualism is difficult due to existing ways of constructing collectives and groups through ethnic and racial belonging which rely on boundaries of inclusion and exclusion. Additionally, mixed people often share more affiliations with others across race, cultural practices, ethnicity, or religion than within the category mixed itself, which, by its very nature, is internally diverse (Lincoln 2008). The category remains unchartered beyond individual understandings of mixedness, although British grassroots organizations are beginning to suggest that mixedness can be a way to form belonging (Intermix, People in Harmony, Mix-d). These ideas engage with the notion that mixedness can be a shared experience of ambiguous appearance and mis-recognition, leading to specific practices to secure social legitimacy and belonging with an emphasis on lived experience as knowledge. Post-race theory moves away from an understanding of identity as fixed, and it is now widely accepted and recognized that race is fluid and multiple and that differences are constructed by and through discursive practices in the environment (Butler 1993). Further, although essentialism is discounted, race becomes reified through discourse and its circulation mediates and informs practices (Gilroy 2000). Identity dominates understandings of mixedness, and this allows social and political factors to be without interrogation, meaning it remains an individualized experience. This individualistic and psychologizing tendency endures in literature and places mixedness as an inherently symptomatic identity.

Mixed Race Identity Development

Much of the existing writing on mixedness tends to veer, firstly, towards mixed as a problematic identity used to explain behavioural problems among young people in care (Okitikpi 2005; Olumide 2002); and secondly, towards an emphasis on racial identity without an overt consideration of gender, ethnicity, sexuality, class, or geographical location (Prevatt-Goldstein 1999; Small 1986). These two approaches assert race a priori and place an over-emphasis on mixedness as inherently problematic as a racial classification and a lived position. Existing research on mixed young people in care focuses on the assumption that a mixed identity is both problematic at the point of racial difference and an untenable social position. For example, research shows that 'mixed parentage children and adolescents in local authority care exhibit identity confusion and low self esteem' (Robinson 2005: 77). The assertion of race a priori negates the complexity of the lives of children and young people in foster care who have often negotiated particularly complex and fraught family circumstances and entered care after traumatic experiences. Mixed young people in care are caught up in complex processes of racialization such that the social and personal complexities of their lives can become reduced to the assumptions made about mixed as an inherently problematic classification.

The American sociologist Robert Park (1931) concluded that the mixed blood or 'marginal man' was predestined to live in two cultures and two worlds, reflective of the binary of race segregation and anti-miscegenation laws of that time and place. Marginal man was therefore capable of a more critical and objective insight into social life and thus more 'intelligent, restless, aggressive and ambitious' (ibid.: 534). Park's colleague Everett Stonequist (1937) claimed inherent psychological maladjustment was also inevitable to marginality, leading to feelings of isolation, alienation, and non-belonging. The solution to such a precarious existence was to become embedded in black cultural and social life, reflecting the rule of hypo-descent or the one-drop law. Tizard and Phoenix (1993: 28) point out that at the time no empirical research was undertaken with mixed people to prove or disprove this hypothesis; however, the legacy of 'marginality' continues through attention to mixed identity as 'crisis, confusion and problems'.

Adolescence is commonly cited, among psychologists, as a time when identity problems or crises occur, and this phase of development has been critically used to examine the development of 'racial identity' among young people (Tizard and Phoenix 1993: 29). Models of identity which outline a linear trajectory, such as Eriksson's (1980) eight-stage model, state that the adolescent becomes so secure in their identity that upon reaching adult-hood they need never think through identity again. The mature adult identity is understood to be so resilient as not to experience affronts as dam-aging to self-esteem, leading to distress or confusion. Similarly, Cross (1971, 1991) suggests a five-stage model of racial development of 'Nigrescence in Afro-Americans', the stages of which culminate in an 'internalisation of and commitment to negriscence' (cited in Katz and Treacher 2005: 53). In these two models there is an end point to identity, which is arrived at either by maturity or acceptance. However, the model of negriscence 'does not include the possibility of integrating more than one racial or ethnic group identity into one's sense of self' (Robinson 2000: 20) and cannot be applied to mixedness. Further, Cohen's (1994: 67–68) critique of the positive black identity model urges a consideration of the reflection of a teleological view of black history as an onward and upward march; and, in this context, a sense of unity and coherency in relation to identity reflects struggles for black independence. Understandings of identity as fluid, multiple, and situ-ational contend with the more orthodox views of identity cited by Eriksson and Cross which have specific trajectories and culminate in specific end points, and such models would declare that 'children who display inconsis-tent identities [are] mixed up' (Katz and Treacher 2005: 53–54).

Song (2003) approaches mixed racial and ethnic identity as a cyclical journey in which there is no end point of maturation or commitment to one race; instead multifaceted and fluid ideas of identity are practised. Root (1996) developed a model specifically with mixed or multiracial people at the forefront, acknowledging the intersectional and situational nature of identity and not separating race as a phenomenon outside of other variables, such as class, gender, disability, and sexual orientation. She also acknowledges that identity is formed in the context of individual, family, and community relationships. Mixedness is considered through connections to others and how these social relations impact on understandings and development of the self. There is a focus on wholeness and a move away from splitting mixed people into separate races or identifications, and she asks: '[h]ow exactly does a person be one fourth, one eighth, or one half of something?' (Root 1996: 3) The idea of splitting and separation emerges from earlier views of race as a form of purity and also draws from the one-drop law commonly used for economic exploitation in the USA. These positions on identity as cyclical, intersectional, and situational are more useful to define the experience of mixedness as it shifts through specific contexts and identity becomes a performance. However, children and young people in foster care are separated from familial sources of identity and thus offer insightful ways to understand how identity is practised.

Understanding mixedness among young people living with their birth families suggests racial identity is no more problematic for mixed young people than it is for others (Ali 2003; Tizard and Phoenix 1993; Wilson 1987). Of the mixed children in the Wilson study, 14 % claimed a white identity, 8 % claimed black, 20 % were inconsistent, and 59 % said they were coloured, half-caste, or half and half. Some took a black identity outside of the family and a mixed one within it 'without perceiving a contradiction between the two' (Wilson 1987: vi). However, Song (2003: 60) claims that the private/public split in this model generates a concern about the meaningfulness of a dual notion of identity 'if it is not recognized or legitimated in social interactions with others'. Root (1992) claims that identity anchors the child within the family and this extends beyond to school and friendships. Root (1992) also claims that while race and ethnicity may be important, they are not necessarily dominant. Ali (2003) agrees, and in her study among a group of eight to eleven year old children living in birth families she stated that '"race" is not always the most salient factor in their lives … what they are really concerned about is, "colourism, culturism and nationalism"'. Lived experiences of children for whom race is a factor give meaning through how they choose to look, dress, and talk (Ali 2003: 180–181).

These studies suggest mixed children and young people do inhabit both black and mixed identities, as both Wilson (1987) and Tizard and Phoenix (1993) claim. This racial positioning has been theorized by Anzaldúa (1987) as a border identity between two established social categories incorporating both blackness and whiteness into a unique self-referential hybrid category. Some mixed people stress their 'multiple and fluid identities and membership of various ethnic groups simultaneously' (Song 2003: 66). Counter to fixed models of identity development, these studies suggest that a range of strategies are utilized by young people to inform their identification practices within their families and wider community. For mixed children in foster care, 'identity' is formed outside of birth families and often without stability or community support, and it is this structuring of the mixed family which placement planning aims to replicate in order for an appropriate mixed race identity to be developed.

References

Ali, S. (2003). *Mixed-race, post-race: Gender, new ethnicities and cultural practices*. Oxford: Berg.

Alibhai-Brown, Y. (2001). *Mixed feelings: The complex lives of mixed race Britons*. London: The Women's Press.

Anzaldúa, G. (1987). *Borderlands/La Frontera: The new mestiza*. San Francisco, CA: Aunt Lute Books.

Aspinall, P. (2009). Does the British state categorisation of mixed race meet public policy needs? *Social Policy and Society, 9*(1), 55–69.

Aspinall, P. J., & Song, M. (2013). *Mixed race identities*. Basingstoke: Palgrave Macmillan.

Banks, N. (1995). Children of Black mixed parentage and their placement needs. *Fostering and Adoption, 19*(2), 19–24.

Barn, R. (1993). *Black children in the public care system*. London: Batsford.

Barn, R. (1999). White mothers, mixed-parentage children and child welfare. *British Journal of Social Work, 29*, 269–284.

Barn, R. (2011). Care leavers and social capital: understanding and negotiating racial and ethnic identity. In T. Reynolds (Ed.), *Young people, social capital and ethnic identity* (pp. 85–102). London: Routledge.

Barn, R., Andrew, L., & Mantovani, N. (2005). *Life after care: A study of the experiences of young people from different ethnic groups*. York: Joseph Rowntree Foundation.

Barn, R., & Harman, V. (2006). A contested identity: An exploration of the competing social and political discourse concerning the identification and positioning of young people of inter-racial parentage. *British Journal of Social Work, 36*(8), 1309–1324.

Barnes, G. (2004a). *Family therapy in changing times*. Basingstoke: Palgrave Macmillan.

Barnes, J. (2004b). *Place and parenting: A study of four communities: The relevance of community characteristics and residents perceptions of their neighbourhoods for parenting and child behaviour in four contrasting locations* (Final report for the families and neighbourhoods study (FANS) submitted to the NSPCC. Part 1: Quantitative results). London: NSPCC.

Bauman, Z. (1996). From pilgrim to tourist—Or a short history of identity. In S. Hall & P. Du Gay (Eds.), *Questions of cultural identity* (pp. 18–36). London: Sage.

Bebbington, A., & Miles, J. (1989). The background of children who enter local authority care. *British Journal of Social Work, 19*(5), 349–368.

Bebbington, A., & Miles, J. (1990). The supply of foster families for children in care. *British Journal of Social Work, 20*(4), 283–307.

Bratter, J. (2007). Will 'multiracial' survive to the next generation? The racial classification of multiracial parents. *Social Forces, 86*(2), 821–849.

Briggs, F., & Hawkins, R. M. F. (1996). To what extent can child protection programmes keep children safe? In N. J. Taylor & A. B. Smith (Eds.), *Investing in children: Primary prevention strategies*, 45–66. Dunedin: Children Issues Centre, University of Otago.

Brown, G. W., & Harris, T. (1978). *Social origins of depression: A study of psychiatric disorder in women*. London: Tavistock Publications.

Butler, J. (1993). *Bodies that matter: On the discursive limits of 'sex'*. London: Routledge.

Caballero, C., Edwards, R., & Puthussery, S. (2008). *Parenting 'mixed' children: Negotiating difference and belonging in mixed race, ethnicity and faith families*. London: Joseph Rowntree Foundation.

Camper, C. (2004). Into the mix. In J. O. Ifekwunigwe (Ed.), *Mixed race studies: A reader*. London: Routledge.

Cleaver, E. (1968). *Soul on ice*. New York: McGraw-Hill.

Cohen, P. (1994). Yesterday's words, tomorrow's world: From the racialisation of adoption to the politics of difference. In I. Gaber & J. Aldridge (Eds.), *Culture, identity and transracial adoption: In the best interests of the child*. London: Free Association Books. http://philcohenworks.com/pcowwp/wp-content/uploads/Phil-Cohen-YESTERDAYS-WORDS.website.pdf

Cross, W. E. (1971). The Negro to Black conversion experience: Toward a psychology of Black liberation. *Black World, 20*, 13–27.

Cross, W. (1991). *Shades of Black: Diversity in African American identity*. Philadelphia, PA: Temple University Press.

DaCosta, K. (2009). *Making multiracials: State, family and market in the redrawing of the color line*. Stanford, CA: Stanford University Press.

Dearing, E., McCartney, K., & Taylor, B. (2004). Change in family income-to-needs matters more for children with less. In NICHD Early Child Care Research Network (Ed.), *Child care and child development: Results from the NICHD study of early childcare and youth development*. New York: Guildford publications.

Dewan, I. A. (2008). *Recasting race: Women of mixed heritage in further education*. Stoke-on-Trent: Trentham Books.

Duck, S. (Ed.). (1993). *Social context of relationships*. Newbury Park, CA: Sage.

Erikson, E. (1980). *Identity and the life cycle*. London: Norton.

Fanon, F. (1968). *Black skin, white masks*. London: Mac Gibbon and Kee.

Ferguson, I. L. (1982). *Fantastic experiences of a half-blind and his interracial marriage: An autobiography*. San Francisco, CA: Lunan-Ferguson.

Foucault, M. (1977). *Discipline and punish: The birth of the prison*. London: Penguin Books.

Frankenberg, R. (1997). *Displacing whiteness: Essays on social and cultural criticism*. Durham, NC: Duke University Press.

Frost, N., Mills, S., & Stein, M. (1999). *Understanding residential child care*. Aldershot: Ashgate Arena.

Gallagher, C. A. (2004). Racial redistricting: Expanding the boundaries of whiteness. In H. Dalmage (Ed.), *The politics of multiculturalism: Challenging racial thinking* (pp. 59–76). New York: New York University Press.

Gill, A. (1995). *Ruling passions: Sex, race and empire*. London: BBC Books.

Gillies, V. (2007). *Marginalised mothers: Exploring working-class experiences of parenting*. London: Routledge.

Gilroy, P. (2000). *Between camps: Nations, culture and the allure of race*. London: Penguin Books.

Hester, M., Pearson, C., & Harwin, N. (2000). *Making an impact: Children and domestic violence. A Reader*. London: Jessica Kingsley.

Holt, T. C. (2002). *The problem of race in the 21st century* (2nd ed.). Cambridge, MA: Harvard University Press.

Ifekwunigwe, J. O. (1999). *Scattered belongings: Cultural paradoxes of race, nation and gender*. London: Routledge.

Kannan, C. T. (1973). *Interracial marriages in London: A comparative study*. London: CT Press.

Katz, I. (1996). *The construction of racial identity in children of mixed parentage: Situating race and racisms*. London: Jessica Kingsley.

Katz, I., Corlyon, J., La Placa, V., & Hunter, S. (2007). *The relationship between parenting and poverty*. London: Joseph Rowntree Foundation.

Knowles, C. (1996). *Family boundaries: The invention of normality and dangerousness*. Peterborough, ON: Broadview Press.

Knowles, C. (2003). *Race and social analysis*. London: Sage.

Lincoln, B. (2008). *Mix-d: UK: A look at mixed-race identities*. Manchester: Pelican Press.

Mahtani, M. (2005). Mixed metaphors: Positioning "mixed-race" identity. In *Situating "race" and racisms in space, time, and theory* (pp. 77–93). Canada, ON: McGill-Queen's University Press.

Mama, A. (1995). *Beyond the masks: Race, gender and subjectivity*. London: Routledge.

Marsh, A., & Mackay, S. (1994). *Poor smokers*. London: Policy Studies Institute.

Massey, D. (1994). *Space, place and gender*. Minneapolis, MN: University of Minneapolis Press.

Masson, J. M., Pearce, J., Bader, K., Joyner, O., Marsden, J., & Westlake, D. (2008). *Care profiling study* (Ministry of Justice Research Series 4/08). London: Ministry of Justice.

Maximé, J. (1993). The importance of racial identity for the psychological well-being of Black children. *Association for Child Psychology and Psychiatry Review and Newsletter, 15*(4), 173–179.

McKenney, N. R., & Bennett, C. E. (1994). Issues regarding data on race and ethnicity: The Census Bureau experience. *Public Health Reports, 109*(1), 16–25.

Mckenzie, L. (2009). *Finding value on a council estate: complex lives, motherhood, and exclusion*. PhD Thesis, Nottingham University.

Miles, R. (1989). *Racism*. London: Routledge.

Morley, D., & Street, C. (2014). *Mixed experiences: Growing up mixed race – mental health and well-being*. London: National Children's Bureau.

Nassy Brown, J. (2005). *Dropping anchor, setting sail: Geographies of race in Black Liverpool*. Oxford: Princeton University Press.

Okitikpi, T. (Ed.). (2005). *Working with children of mixed parentage*. In Okitikpi (Ed.) Dorset: Russell House.

Olumide, J. (2002). *Raiding the gene pool: The social construction of mixed race*. London: Pluto Press.

Owen, C. (2001). Mixed race in official statistics. In D. Parker and M. Song (Eds.), *Rethinking 'mixed race'* (pp. 134–153). London: Pluto Press.

Owen, C. (2007). Statistics: The mixed category in Census 2001. In J. Sims (Ed.), *Mixed heritage: Identity, policy, practice* (pp. 1–5). London: Runnymede Trust.

Owen, C., & Statham, J. (2009). *Disproportionality in child welfare: The prevalence of Black and ethnic minority children within the 'looked after' and 'children in need' populations and on child protection registers in England*. London: Thomas Coram Research Unit, Institute of Education.

Owusu-Bempah, J. (2005). Mulatto man, half-caste, mixed race: The one-drop rule in professional practice. In T. Okitikpi (Ed.), *Working with children of mixed parentage*. Dorset: Russell House.

Park, R. (1931). The mentality of racial hybrids. *American Journal of Sociology, 36*, 534–551.

Parker, D., & Song, M. (2001). *Rethinking 'mixed race'*. London: Pluto Press.

Patel, N., & Fatimilehin, I. (2005). Racism and clinical psychology: Has anything changed? *Clinical Psychology, 48*(May). http://www.justpsychology.co.uk/node/47

Pelton, L. H. (2015). The continuing role of material factors in child maltreatment and placement. *Child Abuse Neglect, 41*, 30–39. doi:10.1016/j.chiabu.2014.08.001. Epub 2014 Aug 26.

Peters, F. (2010). *Who cares about mixed race? Experiences of young people in an inner city borough*. Unpublished PhD thesis, University of London.

Prevatt-Goldstein, B. (1999). Direct work with Black children with one White parent. In R. Barn (Ed.), *Working with Black children and adolescents in need*. London: BAAF.

Radford, L., & Hester, M. (2006). *Mothering through domestic violence*. London: Jessica Kingsley.

Robinson, L. (2000). The racial identity attitudes and self-esteem of Black adolescents in residential care: An exploratory study. *British Journal of Social Work, 30*(1), 3–24.

Robinson, L. (2005). Practice issues: Working with children of mixed parentage. In T. Okitikpi (Ed.), *Working with children of mixed parentage*. Dorset: Russell House.

Rockquemore, K. A., & Brunsma, D. (2002). *Beyond Black: Biracial identity in America*. Thousand Oaks, CA: Sage.

Root, M. P. (Ed.). (1992). *Racially mixed people in America*. Newbury Park, CA: Sage.

Root, M. P. (1996). *The multiracial experience*. Newbury Park, CA: Sage.

Selwyn, J. Harris, P., Quinton, D. Nawaz, S., Wijedasa, D., & Wood, M. (2008). *Pathways to permanence for black, Asian and mixed ethnicity children: Dilemmas, decision-making and outcomes*. Bristol: Hadley Centre for Adoption and Foster Care Studies, University of Bristol.

Skeggs, B. (1997). *Formations of class and gender*. London: Sage.

Small, J. (1986). Transracial placement: Conflict and contradiction. In S. Ahmed, J. Cheetham, & J. Small (Eds.), *Social work with Black children and their families*. London: BAAF.

Solomos, J., & Back, L. (1996). *Racism and society*. Basingstoke: Palgrave Macmillan.

Song, M. (2003). *Choosing ethnic identity*. Cambridge: Polity Press.

Song, M. (2010). Does 'race' matter? A study of 'mixed race' siblings' identifications. *The Sociological Review, 58*(2), 265–285.

Spencer, R. (2006). *Challenging multiracial identity*. Boulder, CO: Lynne Rienner Publishers.

Stoler, A. (1995). Mixed bloods and the cultural politics of European identity in colonial Southeast Asia. In J. N. Pieterse & B. Parekh (Eds.), *The decolonisation of the imagination: Culture, knowledge and power*. London: Zed Books.

Stonequist, E. (1937). *The marginal man: A study in personality and culture conflict*. New York: Charles Scribner's Sons.

Thoburn, J. (2005). Permanent family placement for children of dual heritage: Issues arising from a longitudinal study. In T. Okitikpi (Ed.), *Working with children of mixed parentage*. Dorset: Russell House.

Thoburn, J., Norford, L., & Rashid, S. P. (2000a). *Permanent family placement for children of minority ethnic origin*. London: Jessica Kingsley.

Thoburn, J., Wilding, J., & Watson, J. (2000b). *Family support in cases of emotional abuse and neglect*. London: The Stationery Office.

Tizard, B., & Phoenix, A. (1993). *Black, White or mixed race?: Race and racism in the lives of young people of mixed parentage*. London: Routledge.

Townsend, P. (1979). *Poverty in the United Kingdom: A survey of household resources and standards of living*. Harmondsworth: Penguin.

Twine, F. W. (1999a). Bearing blackness in Britain: The meaning of racial difference from White birth mothers of African descent children. *Social Identities, 5*(2), 185–210.

Twine, F. W. (1999b). Transracial mothering and antiracism: The case of White birth mothers of Black children in Britain. *Feminist Studies, 25*(3), 729–746.

Vertovec, S. (2007). Superdiversity and its implications. *Ethnic and Racial Studies, 30*(6), 1024–1054.

Wade, P. (1993). *Blackness and race mixture: The dynamics of racial identity in Colombia.* Baltimore, MD: Johns Hopkins University Press.

Ware, V., & Back, L. (2002). *Out of whiteness: Color, politics and culture.* London: University of Chicago Press.

Wilson, A. (1987). *Mixed race children: A study of identity.* London: Allen and Unwin.

Websites

The Children Act 1989. http://www.opsi.gov.uk/acts/acts1989/ukpga_19890041_en_4

US data on children in care and multiracial children. https://www.childwelfare.gov/pubPDFs/foster.pdf

www.baaf.org/node/7634 (accessed on 12 October 2015).

www.womensaid.org.uk/domestic-violence-articles (accessed on 20 December 2008).

https://www.gov.uk/government/publications/children-looked-after-return-2015-to-2016-guide

Visual Media

Harry Enfield and Chums. (1994–1997).

4

Researching Mixedness as a Category of Experience

The central questions of this book are:

- How do young people make meaning from the discursive repertoires of the mixed classification in their care experiences?
- In what ways are care experiences being structured through understandings of mixedness?

Approaches to race are mediated through its awkwardness as an enduring social category premised upon the body, twinned with the recognition that race has a real impact on and is a serious consequence for individuals. The first problem of defining mixedness then becomes part of the recognition that race exists and is thus meaningful in social life and that mixed people are somehow the sum of two disparate and irreconcilable parts of a whole. Yet, this understanding is critiqued by critical mixed studies, which ask how and why one ought to be split into two or more parts and whether race is in fact useful or if its abandonment would be more fruitful. The second consideration of mixedness concerns whether or not it can be theorized beyond the individual, since defining mixed as an ethnic group relies upon processes of inclusion and exclusion. This

© The Editor(s) (if applicable) and The Author(s) 2016
F. Peters, *Fostering Mixed Race Children*,
DOI 10.1057/978-1-137-54184-0_4

then leads us into asking who can be mixed and how that can then be defined without invoking race through essentialism. The dilemma for mixed young people in care is that these problems of definition inform the constructions of their care experiences and the practices they engender, which impact in specific ways with adverse consequences for their care experiences. Such experiences of mixedness can become even more peculiar to the young people through the ways in which Children's Social Care processes and foster care act upon racialization through discursive repertoires of race. Such experiences are the focus of this book and explore the problem through attention to its constitutive parts (care processes) and its constituents (care experiences) in order to examine what is peculiar about being mixed and in care.

Everyday Experience Is Knowledge

Investigations of experience among groups with a common racial or ethnic classification can often lead to groups being said to share a unitary experience brought about through their shared social location. Conversely, racial categories can produce 'dominant, fixed, homogeneous ideas about the individuals within those categories' (Gunaratnam 2003: 28). An interrogation of this position has allowed experience to be opened up to claims that a deeper understanding of how categories construct experience is required (Lewis 2000). The achievement of this, through an examination of the meanings attached to race, gender, class, and age at various moments and deconstruction of categories and classifications of groups, has renewed knowledge production as both experiential and situated. The boundaries of experience are constituted through attention to the impact these categories have on social relations and how they are made meaningful through social interaction, within the organizational practices and everyday interactions they engender. Utilizing mixed as a classification in Children's Social Care reveals how processes of race-making bring about diversity within the mixed classification and reveal its 'inadequacy as a single and coherent category' (Ali 2003: 5).

Mixed race as a category is a shifting, political, and symbolic classification and cannot be easily fixed to produce specific, neat conceptualizations of experience (Olumide 2002). Keith (2005: 4) suggests that 'race, ethnicity and identity cannot be taken for granted as objects to be studied, precisely because their meanings are context dependent'. It is more useful to place an emphasis on racialization in situ to examine how mixed, as a category, operates across the organizational practices of Children's Social Care. In this way 'how we act upon classification in everyday practices and how we are positioned within a racial order' can emerge through attention to experience (Ware and Back 2002: 124). Racialization in situ offers a way to conceptualize race, ethnicity, and culture as flexible, contestable, and shifting, depending on the location being studied. Racialization operates through people in specific social sites and is embodied and acted upon by others. The mixed classification operates within other embodied readings such as class, gender, and education, and all these factors taken together discern layers of meaning through social practices and the everyday experiences those practices precipitate.

Theoretically, race has dubious underpinnings in terms of pseudoscientific claims to essential differences among human populations, and these have been discounted. However, race has social consequences with particular manifestations, expressions, and outcomes located in specific places and mobilized in specific ways according to the logic of the site. Duster (cited in Twine 2000: xii) states, 'there are those who argue that just to acknowledge race, is to perpetuate the biological myth of race. But, this is to confuse the biological with the social.' People make race meaningful across all types of social and institutional discourses, and race structures lives in real ways (Knowles 2003). Studying the social construction and racialization of the mixed classification in the site of foster care can build insights into processes of race-making and how these structure the experiences of young people.

Research with young people in care confirms that 'distressed young people or those in transition may not want to be involved in research' (Connolly et al. 2006: 62). The lives of the young people in care are complex, and the participants do not reflect the full range of experiences and complexity of foster care; they all have stable, secure placements with foster families and are settled at school. They present few problems in terms of behaviour. They are too perfect. However, a year is a long time and there are changes that perhaps would have resulted in their de-selection. Previous research with children and young people in care (Thomas and O'Kane 1998) highlights the practice of social workers acting as gatekeepers and excluding young people from making decisions to participate in research. Their right to make decisions over their participation remains crucial, particularly within a care system that works to protect and uphold children's rights. The United Nations Convention declares that children have the right to participate in decisions that affect them. Article 12 states, 'every child who is capable of forming his or her own views must have the right to express those views freely in all matters affecting the child' (Cloke and Davies 1995: 29). Care Matters: Time to Deliver also campaigns for looked-after children to enjoy the same rights as children living with parents (www.dcsf.gov.uk, 2008). The right to participate in decisions is not contingent on a judgement about the child's competence or restricted by an adult's perception of their best interests (Thomas and O'Kane 1998). The dissonance between policy and legislation and its implementation at the level of individual social workers can have an adverse impact on the way in which children in care make their own decisions about their contribution to their lives.

Racialization and Identifying Mixedness

> I can think of a child for you … she's mixed race; she says she's black and she denies her white, you know … she doesn't want to talk about the white side, but you can see it, you know, when you look at her. (Social Worker, March, 2008)

Race works through visual grammar; how we look matters and classification practices are subject to individual understandings of what mixed looks like and how it ought to operate in an existing racial schema. The numerous permutations of the mixed race classification and the ethnic affiliations within mixedness point to the complexity of working with racial classifications and to the open, contestable nature of it as a classification. Mixedness is understood by social workers as an ambiguous social location in which a number of affiliations could be made. They have the task of classifying the young people they work with using both ethnic heritage and visual appearance. The complexity and variation within the mixed race category illuminate how group identities deconstruct race. It is impossible to close down mixedness in familiar terms, for example through the closed boundaries of race or ethnicity. Mixed as an ethnic classification confirms the poststructuralist concern with acknowledging 'erasures and exclusions at the level of categorization' (Gunaratnam 2003: 31). Mixed heritage and the ethnic differences within the category have to be flattened or erased in order to encompass those who were defined as mixed by social workers. Reducing mixedness a priori to race reaffirms essentialist identities in a way that denies complex subjectivity and ignores the lived ways that people negotiate their multiple and shifting identifications. Investigating a range of other identifications and paying attention to the personal biographies of the participants allows the lived experience of mixedness to be prioritized.

> Mixed race people are said to occupy an in between status that may lead to earlier race consciousness. (Brackett et al. 2006)

It is the experience of mixedness that becomes integrated and lived within the site of foster homes and the regulatory processes of the care system. Such an approach integrates a diverse range of identifications, and what emerges is the opportunity to examine how mixedness can be conceptualized beyond racial identity or boundaries of ethnic inclusion and exclusion. Despite the difficulty of definition (given its diversity and whether all mixed people could be said to experience their mixedness in similar ways), mixedness is a lived experience that can be investigated through attention to themes of ambiguity, misrecognition, and social legitimacy.

The recommendation of identity work as an intervention process to correct inherent difficulties underpins reasons for some young people becoming participants. Mixedness is also spoken of in ways that racialize it as a repository to explain complexities in young people's lives through inherent difficulties of mixed identity such as behaviour, issues of belonging or fitting in, and rebelliousness. Empirical research by Owusu-Bempah (1994) describes the findings of an exercise in which trainee social workers are given three case studies of boys with behavioural problems, one white, one black, and one mixed race. The social workers' task is to assess the core causes of the boys' problems and their intervention needs. Among the social workers 85 % of the respondents attribute the mixed race boy's problems to his identity needs, as opposed to 59 % for the black boy, and 25 % for the white boy. Katz and Treacher (2005: 45) argue that 'overt attention to the identity needs of mixed young people often fails to consider a wider attention to needs'. Psychologizing tendencies defer personal problems present among individuals and attempt to solve them with attention to difficulties the individual may have managing social life—rather than paying attention to inequalities of social life and linking those to manifestations of personal difficulties. A lack of attention to social forces and processes of discrimination then locates those problems within the individual/group most afflicted by them. Care admission rates of mixed race children signal a breakdown in social process not due to an inherent dysfunction of mixing or mixedness in and of itself.

Emotional Research and Researching Emotions

There are things that I'm interested in that people don't bring up. And I feel that sometimes I can't bring them up because I really want to get at what people think is important to talk about. So I take from what people say; that's where all my questions come from, just how people talk. (Nassy Brown 2005: 223)

The qualitative interview is an opportunity to talk through an agenda and is part of the interpretative tradition that believes in a rational and knowing subject who is able to 'tell it like it is' (Hollway and Jefferson 2000: 3). The attempt to locate the expression of our many selves within a matrix of social relations is often undone by thematic research agendas using question and answer formats that leave participants the task of conjuring up cold, hard answers from a range of pre-determined themes. Much of the supporting role in true participation is uncomfortable and leads to a feeling of wanting to take back control and impose a structure in order to standardize responses and minimize uncertainty. Judgement calls about what is fitting and professional compete with demands of ethical and participatory research. Decisions have to be made on the spot using intuitive insight, trusting the participants to know their limitations and their lives. Social research with young people in care is an ethical minefield of on-the-spot judgements about safety, welfare, and support that entail a high level of engagement to guide safe explorations of life stories in all their complexity.

> Participatory action research can help children construct their everyday experiences into knowledge, gain self-confidence in their abilities and influence decisions that are taken about their lives. (Fraser et al. 2004: 207)

The gathering of narrative data owes much to Hollway and Jefferson (2000); the technique of free association 'widens access to a subjects experiences and meaning' (ibid.: 155). However, this interpretation and analysis does not delve into unconscious inter-subjectivity, nor does it develop a detailed profile of participants or their motivations or desires that drive their actions or preferred identity. 'The associations follow pathways defined by emotional motivations, rather than rational intentions' (Hollway and Jefferson 2000: 37). The usefulness of personal narrative is that it can 'extrapolate ... to the broader social location embodied by the individual' (McCall 2005: 1781). Most of the talk is generated by the participants, and in this way a much larger range of themes are discussed, not all of them relating to care but to what is active at that time in their lives, such as friendships, siblings, family, events, or school.

> I want to show you where I used to live, and the school I used to go to, the places that I've been, that I can tell stories about. (Amma, July: 2008)

The Biographic Interpretive Method is useful in understanding and interpreting the dissonance between the 'lived life' and the 'story told' (Wengraf 2001: 144). What we experience in the world and what we are willing to tell others is understood in the context of our accumulated knowledge of the social world and locates multiple positions as a particular kind of social being (Chamberlayne et al. 2000). Narrative analysis is considered an alternative to scientific understanding of the individual abstracted from context. Putting the subject in context through the narrative study of lives combines both life experience and identity connected to social groupings, situations, and events (Josselson and Lieblich 1998). In this method free association allows the anxieties and defences that arise in the participants to become a narrative that reveals the whole person—their Gestalt. Wertheimer, the founder of 'Gestalt', believes that the whole is greater than the sum of its parts and that in understanding 'the structure we shall need to have insight into it. There is then some possibility that the components themselves will be understood' (cited in Murphy and Kovach 1972: 258–259). The opportunity to produce and construct knowledge, to give it meaning, and to share that meaning with others can be 'transformative for the participant' and is an aspect of research reciprocity (Denzin 1989: 17). Life narratives can be a catalyst enabling us to 'interrogate, evaluate, disrupt', or even overturn narratives in order to promote positive and creative change (Holland et al. 2008: 21).

There is awareness that traumatic and repressed memories may emerge, as all of the participants have been affected by birth family and foster care experiences. Using image production is a process to enable and facilitate talking, and this offers further understanding of process and not production. The visual narratives are often not purposive but emerge through the camera's ability to show absence and presence through production.

> Place is to everyday interaction what social status is to social structure. That is while a status is a socially agreed upon, macro-level position, a place is less well defined, micro-level position such as follower, leader, star, supporting character … the concept of place encompasses differences in what sociologists have called power, prestige, face-to-face status, and social distance. (Clark 1990: 306)

In emotional research, place engages with the micro-politics of interaction to subvert social status within the shifting terrain of claims, whereby an offer of sympathy, born out of a caring ethic, can clash with the commitment to participation and leadership. During a conversation with Amma, in which she recounts abuse at home and in foster care, my response is to apologize for the wrongs against her. Interestingly, and in line with Clark's (1990) emphasis, she rejects my response of sympathy and retorts, 'You don't need to be sorry—it's not your fault.' In doing so she asserts her place as more powerful than the victim of abuse status I had offered. Clark's (1990) analysis goes on to suggest that offering sympathy can be a way of establishing superiority, yet the receiver may not accept sympathy as a strategy to refuse the problem 'because it acknowledges failure to control either oneself or the environment' (ibid.: 325). In this scenario of place and empathy between researcher and participant, the assumption that the social status of an adult, professional researcher always holds the power in research relationships with young people can be overturned in ways that highlight the nature of participation. Mediating the relationship in this environment of child protection carries its own risks and raises issues about my own professional vulnerability.[1]

The parallel between therapy and research is clear as the researcher often uncovers hidden, painful, or deeply complex memories or feelings. Such disclosures tend to deepen relationships between the people involved (Lee 1993). A healthy sense of reciprocity, an engagement with their dilemmas, and an approach with an emphasis on caring is the most productive way to proceed. There is some consensus that a longitudinal approach when collating data from children and young people yields greater quality of data (Jones and Tannock 2000).

The hermeneutic craft of intuiting, or spending time dwelling on the text, analyzing the meaning of the things, and writing a full description, is the key analytical method. Moustakas (1990) claims that researchers engage in a journey of discovery too, which draws on their capacity to learn and know, stating that qualitative discoveries cannot be forced, as they emerge through waiting and patience. The stories the young people tell are interpreted by an approach to narratives that informs 'the ways in which we make and use knowledge to create and preserve our social worlds and our places within them' (Fook 2002: 132). Treating the narrative as a topic to be explored often points to and engages with how specific types of identity are performed as co-productions (Hollway and Jefferson 2000). The analysis is rich in meaning; it is diverse and representative of the young people's experiences in all their wholeness—their Gestalt. The whole in this instance, as outlined by Hollway and Jefferson (2000: 69), also refers to 'all I have accumulated relating to a particular person who took part in the research'. These ephemera are transcripts, memories of meetings, field work diaries, meetings with other people who the participant knows and what was said about them, back stories from social

[1] My research project adheres to guidelines set out by the British Sociological Association and defers to the ethics statement of the Economic and Social Research Council (ESRC). The project refers to the guidelines for working with children set out by Barnardo's. The storage, use, and disclosure of data are within the Data Protection Act 1998.

workers and foster carers, observations, and random interactions of which I was a part. Gestalt refers most broadly to holding all of these things in mind to retrieve (primarily through awareness, close attention to, and immersion in transcripts) intuition and attention to the participants. The case study lets 'readers discover what is there that can be applied to their own situation and what cannot' (Hollway and Jefferson, 2000: 93). Qualitative data with children offers detailed information yet this is solely a product of both time and place of both researchers and those who participate in research and is thus difficult to generalize (Jones and Tannock 2000: 93). The validity of the data is robust and is representative of the specific space, time, relationships, and circumstances.

References

Ali, S. (2003). *Mixed-race, post-race: Gender, new ethnicities and cultural practices.* Oxford: Berg.

Brackett, K. P., Marcus, A., McKenzie, N. J., Mullins, L. C., Tang, Z., & Allen, A. M. (2006). The effects of multiracial identification on students' perceptions of racism. *The Social Science Journal, 43*, 437–444.

Chamberlayne, P., Bornat, J., & Wengraf, T. (2000). *The turn to biographical methods in social science: Comparative issues and examples.* London: Routledge.

Clark, C. (1990). Emotions and micropolitics in everyday life: Some patterns and paradoxes of "place." In T. D. Kemper (Ed.), Research agendas in the sociology of emotions (SUNY Series in the Sociology of Emotions, pp. 305–333, vi, 335 pp). Albany, NY: State University of New York Press.

Cloke, C., & Davies, M. (1995). *Participation and empowerment in child protection.* London: Pitman Publishing.

Connolly, M., Crichton-Hill, Y., & Ward, T. (2006). *Culture and child protection: Reflexive responses.* London: Jessica Kingsley.

Denzin, N. K. (1989). The sociological interview. In N. K. Denzin (Ed.), *The research act* (3rd ed., pp. 102–120). Englewood Cliffs, NJ: Prentice Hall.

Fook, J. (2002). *Social work critical theory and practice.* London: Sage.

Fraser, S., Lewis, V., Ding, S., Kellett, M., & Robinson, C. (2004). *Doing research with children and young people.* London: Sage.

Gunaratnam, Y. (2003). *Researching race and ethnicity: Methods knowledge power.* London: Sage.

Holland, S., Renold, E., Ross, N., & Hillman, A. (2008). *The everyday lives of children in care* (Working Paper-qualiti/WPS/005). University of Cardiff.

Hollway, W., & Jefferson, T. (2000). *Doing qualitative research differently free association, narrative and the interview method*. London: Sage.

Jones, C., & Tannock, J. (2000). A matter of life and death: A reflective account of two examples of practitioner research into children's understanding of death and bereavement. In A. Lewis & G. Lindsay (Eds.), *Researching children's perspectives*. Buckingham: Open University Press.

Josselson, R., & Lieblich, A. (1998). *Exploring identity and gender: The narrative study of lives*. Thousand Oaks, CA: Sage.

Katz, I., & Treacher, A. (2005). The social and psychological development of mixed parentage children. In T. Okitikpi (Ed.), *Working with children of mixed parentage*. Dorset: Russell House.

Keith, M. (2005). *After the cosmopolitan: Multicultural cities and the future of racism*. London: Routledge.

Knowles, C. (2003). *Race and social analysis*. London: Sage.

Lee, R. (1993). *Doing research on sensitive topics*. London: Sage.

Lewis, G. (2000). *Race, gender, social welfare: Encounters in a post-colonial society*. London: Polity Press.

McCall, L. (2005). The complexity of intersectionality. *Signs: A Journal of Women in Culture and Society, 30*(31), 1771–1800.

Moustakas, C. (1990). *Heuristic research: Design, methodology and applications*. London: Sage.

Murphy, G., & Kovach, J. (1972). *Historical introduction to modern psychology*. New York: Harcourt Brace Jovanovich.

Nassy Brown, J. (2005). *Dropping anchor, setting sail: Geographies of race in Black Liverpool*. Oxford: Princeton University Press.

Olumide, J. (2002). *Raiding the gene pool: The social construction of mixed race*. London: Pluto Press.

Owusu-Bempah, J. (1994). Race, self-identity and social work. *British Journal of Social Work, 24*, 123–136.

Thomas, N., & O'Kane, C. (1998). When children's wishes and feelings clash with their "best interests". *International Journal of Children's Rights, 6*, 137–154.

Twine, F. W. (2000). *Racing research researching race*. New York: New York University Press.

Ware, V., & Back, L. (2002). *Out of Whiteness: Color, politics and culture*. London: University of Chicago Press.

Wengraf, T. (2001). *Qualitative research interviewing: Biographic narrative and semi-structured interviewing*. London: Sage.

5

The First Year in Care and the Matrix of Classifications

Stealth	I've got loads of stuff to think about.
Fiona	So, you only thought about it because we're talking about it?
Stealth	Yeah.
Fiona	Did you expect to be coming into foster care?
Stealth	A bit of a surprise. It wasn't like … it wasn't like Hull beat Arsenal, you see, like probability in math, and it's like even chances. I did think something like that could happen because of the conditions I was living in and, um, I never knew it was going to happen like that. Say you buy a 1962 Rover, some old car you go out driving in it in the winter and there's a possibility that it's going to break down, but you don't think it's just going to stop like that. I knew something eventually would happen, but I didn't know what day, what time.

Stealth's thoughts no longer focus on his earlier living conditions and the uncertainty surrounding his mother's debilitating illness rendering her unable to continue caring for him. His ordinary home life ends abruptly. New thoughts and concerns replace his old rhythms, routines and worries, new ways to understand himself and what it means to be

© The Editor(s) (if applicable) and The Author(s) 2016
F. Peters, *Fostering Mixed Race Children*,
DOI 10.1057/978-1-137-54184-0_5

eleven years old and living in foster care, for the first time. Everyday life for Stealth will now emerge through the systems that govern, administer, and regulate foster care and will shape his childhood and adolescent experiences, leaving a lasting impression.

Guidelines of Children's Social Care underpin the caring and administrative practices of fostering; the dissemination of policy and the expectation that foster carers adhere to it are conditions of care-giving. Stealth's adaptation, and sometimes resistance, to these practices shapes and influences his meaning-making, becoming an integral part of his everyday life. The first year in care is a crucial time for young people as they make the transition from home, and some will nurture the prospect of returning. However, there is widespread acknowledgement among practitioners that children who do not return home within the first year will remain in care until eighteen years of age. From Stealth's position as a child in care, an exploration of the relationships he has with carers and professionals who comprise the 'team around the child', all of whom work within a set of legislation, guidelines, and policy, is the focus of this chapter in the following two ways:

Firstly, the initial stages of care admission and the importance of securing an appropriate foster placement, which considers his mixed classification, reveals the complexity of defining mixedness through ethnic and racial boundaries. Further, how Stealth creates meaningful ethnic and racial identification demonstrates the ambiguous social and cultural location of mixedness in Children's Social Care and in social and popular culture. The emphasis on the construction, socialization, and post-race theorization of mixedness and effectively working with the classification within the foster care setting introduces the central thread running through this and subsequent chapters.

Secondly, Stealth shares his ordinary everyday experience of living within a matrix of regulations that require him to contribute to his 'care life' and wider regulations that evaluate the care system. These processes are outside of any intrinsic meaning in the young person's life and tend to focus on improving the care system itself rather than the quality of life of the child within the system. The demands impact on Stealth's ability to lead an ordinary life and also mediate his relationship with his foster carer, who becomes both a nurturer and administrator of bureaucratic practices. Stealth's narrative of his first year in foster care demonstrates how care processes shape his everyday experience and influence how he makes sense of his racial classification and his childhood.

Stealth was experiencing neglect and, with family support coming only from elderly grandparents, his living conditions were untenable. Supporting families with early and appropriate intervention can often keep families together, which is seen as the best option. His grandparents were not seen as suitable carers, due to their age, and so it appears his admission was somewhat inevitable. Once foster care is thought to be the appropriate choice for a child, their specific biography of religion, racial origin, ethnic, cultural, linguistic background, and emotional needs is given active consideration when placement planning.

Defining Mixedness

Mixed race children experience issues of identity, isolation, family support, and racism that need to be understood by practitioners making assessments. (Morley and Street 2014: 69)

The mixed population is growing fast, with rapidly changing configurations of definition, and older ways of thinking about mixed race through overt attention to a one white parent and one black parent paradigm means that understanding mixedness only through the lens of race has limitations (Ifekwunigwe 1999; Tizard and Phoenix 1993; Wilson 1987). The impact of the mixed classification in Children's Social Care thus far is a confusing, inconsistent, and complex terrain of racialization in which mixed families and their children are caught up. Old adages that mixed children are black, black with a white parent, only black, or only white confirm mixed race as ambiguous. Matching practices are made complex by mixedness as a racial and ethnic category, and ongoing debates over how to classify mixed race children and match them with appropriate families (Barn 1993; Okitikpi 2005; Olumide 2002) illustrate the ambiguity of mixed as a classification.

The care of mixed race children requires an understanding of the construction, socialization, and cultural practices of mixedness beyond racial and ethnic boundaries in which the heterogeneity of mixed families is normative (Edwards et al. 2012). Further, an understanding of mixed families' influence of primary cultural socialization in birth families can offer greater accuracy in placement matching decisions, as this can often underpin belonging more strongly than racial and ethnic heritage.

> Where a placement with a foster carer … is required for a child, if it has not been possible to secure an ideal ethnic, cultural or religious match, all efforts will be made to find a family placement that is as close a match as possible. The placement must meet the assessed needs of the child and the child should not stand out as visibly different. (Local Authority guidelines on Trans-Racial and Trans-Cultural placements, 2010)

The matching guidelines that govern fostering reaffirm assumptions about families looking the same—undermining the legitimacy of mixed race families, but also underpinning assumptions about the ability of white birth mothers and foster carers to parent mixed race children. Most children in mixed families stand out as visibly different. Race politics and the legacy of race thinking underpins both fostering and adoption at either point of tension: either the one-way movement of black children into white homes prevalent in adoption, or, conversely, a reliance on visible appearance to match mixed children in foster placements, without fully considering the child's birth family and the role of white mothers. Creating new ways to understand how mixed race young people *experience* their classification before their care admission offers more effective strategies for planning appropriate foster placements.

Meet Stealth: Mixed Race and Mismatched?

Stealth has spent his first year in foster care in one placement five minutes' walk from his old family home, although his mum has now left the area. Stealth's father lives nearby but has no contact with him. He feels that his elderly grandparents and mum are vulnerable and he takes on the role of carer. The foster family are a Jamaican couple with three children, one of whom still lives at home. Sheila, his carer, says being in care embarrassed him at first, but she feels that he is now getting used to it. Stealth goes along to the Sunday service and youth club with the family and he describes himself as Christian.

My first impressions of Stealth were that he was chatty and was interested in the research but unsure how he could contribute. He is an intelligent boy showing concern about environmental issues and politics. He also has a fear of dogs, which on our first visit to the local park resulted in my having to coax him out of the toilets. I enjoyed interviewing Stealth. We had a good rapport; he had a good sense of humour, loved jokes, and his use of analogies was original, accurate, and inspired.

Fiona   Did anyone give you important advice when you came into foster care?

Stealth   I got no advice, actually. It's a funny story how I found out I was in care. Shall I tell it? I was at primary school in year six. I was in a science lesson. The office lady said 'I'm going to introduce you to some people. I said, 'Oh no, has my granddad died?' She said, 'No'. 'My mum died?' She said, 'No'. 'My grandmother?' She said, 'No'. She said, 'The people in here will explain it' and there was a room in the office and I saw two policemen and my mum's social worker and they explained how I was going to be in care and I thought I was going to be like Tracy Beaker[1] and it was going to be fun. Then I realized, 'Oh no, what am I thinking?' and I got angry, was upset, and they gave me a tissue and took me in the police car to, um, where the social workers were, on the top floor and they were ber [lots] people in the office trying to find me a placement.

Fiona   You waited there while they looked?

Stealth   Yeah. 3 p.m. till 5 p.m. Two hours playing with action men. She said, 'Any particular race?' and I said I would not mind if

---

[1] Tracy Beaker is a fictional and feisty character in Jacqueline Wilson's novel about a girl in a children's home, popular with children and young people and dramatized for BBC1.

	it was American, African, Caribbean, or Australian. I wouldn't mind English the best ones would be cockney, I like cockney ones. They're funny, they're like 'Hello, lovey'. The women are lovely. They smoke and make sandwiches. I like Scottish and Irish.
Fiona	Good. You had a choice.
Stealth	At first, it sounded like they were giving me a choice but when they talked about Sheila, it sounded like they were actually forcing me to do this. They were like 'Wow! We found you the perfect placement very near home. Caribbean people and regular churchgoers'. I said, 'Do I have a choice?' They said, 'You do, but we have to tell you this placement seems so perfect'. I was like, 'Ok'. Then, the cab driver didn't know where number eight was so he went up and down the road.
Fiona	Who were you with?
Stealth	Some nice Australian girl. She was nice, but for some reason she acted too causal, like we was going to Pizza Hut or somewhere. She wasn't like, 'Your placement, I hope it's okay'. She was like, 'Oh, I wonder who will be behind the door, like a mystery'.

Planning care admission in advance with the consent and views of the young person being taken into account is the best way to reduce the impact and loss of family life (Stein 1999). Stealth's mother reaching crisis point quickly, resulting in his emergency care admission despite his feeling that something could happen 'but not knowing when', means he has taken a while to settle at his placement and continues to nurture the desire to return to his family. In arranging a placement, a social worker makes an assessment of needs outlining a package of care, which aims to meet the educational, psychological, health, and parenting needs of the child within an appropriate placement. This could be within foster placements, residential homes, secure accommodation, or friend and family placements known as kinship care. For a young person like Stealth, who experiences an emergency care admission, finding a suitable placement depends upon the availability of carers. The team secure a placement fairly quickly. His foster carer works directly for the local authority and is an economically sound option in a competitive marketplace. Carers often choose to work for private fostering agencies, which demand higher remuneration and are seen as offering greater levels of training and support to carers, but are expensive options for Children's Social Care departments.

Pointing towards the illusion of choice, Stealth notes the limitations on his preference for an 'English cockney family', the very thing that must be guarded against if he is to receive culturally appropriate socialization in foster care. His reference point is possibly the care-giving of his English grandmother and women at school who serve lunch. There is a shortage of African-Caribbean foster carers, and the social worker's relief at securing an appropriate foster family is palpable. Stealth's request for a placement with an English Cockney family is highly unlikely as the Association of Black Social Workers and Allied Professionals (ABSWAP) had gathered support for opposing all transracial adoptions and fostering practices during the 1980s. In taking this position ABSWAP was responding to the developments in social work culture of the often unnecessary removal of children from black families by white social workers. Currently, same race matching practices continue to influence decision-making when placing children in foster care but are no longer part of adoption guidelines (Peters 2012).

Understanding Culture

The discovery of a 'perfect' foster placement is not so perfect for Stealth since Jamaica, despite being part of his ethnic heritage, is unfamiliar to him. His grandfather's ambivalent relationship to his birth home, signalled by his purchase of a 'one-way ticket to England' which has not seen him return since his arrival, and his absent Jamaican father are familiar but elusive. Jamaican cultural practices in his birth family were not a priority and so his placement with a Jamaican foster carer, given his mixedness and his relationship to Jamaica, is ambivalent.

Fiona	I suppose you could learn about Jamaica from Sheila.
Stealth	Yeah most of what I know about Jamaica is actually from her because her family goes to Jamaica a lot and they talk about Jamaica a lot and how it is, so most of what I know is from them talking.
Fiona	Do you have Jamaican food?
Stealth	Yeah, if she's up to it.
Fiona	What do you like to eat?
Stealth	It's spicy and I'm not used to it.
Fiona	So your mum never cooked like that?
Stealth	Nah, my mum could hardly cook because she shakes. My granddad doesn't cook. He will cook beans on toast and put garlic on his food. He doesn't cook especially Jamaican.
Fiona	He really doesn't like Jamaica, does he?
Stealth	One-way ticket to England.

Food, a way to grasp cultural practices, can tell us of our links to community, family, and heritage. Family cultural traditions reside on our dining tables. Stealth dislikes spicy food, as his mum was unable to cook, and his grandfather's disinterest in replicating any Jamaican cultural practices leaves him in a cultural vacuum. His mixed race mum has an English mother and so the transmission of 'food know-how' would be of traditional English fare. France Winddance Twine's (Twine 2010) work examines how white mothers in British mixed families do actively learn to be part of their husband's culture through familial relationships and learn how to cook traditional food for the family. Jamaican food isn't part of Stealth's cultural practice at home and his preference sets him apart from his foster family, with mealtimes made tricky by his dislike of spicy food. Matching guidelines demarcate culture without exploring practices in the birth family—ethnic heritage does not always translate into cultural practice—and this primary socialization underpins how young people think about and develop an awareness of belonging. Stealth's awareness of belonging through cultural practices reveals the tension between his ethnicity and cultural knowledge, and his education about Jamaican culture really begins in foster care, despite it being part of his heritage.

The value of ethnicity and culture was fought for during the 1980s by ABSWAP to ensure that black children in residential and foster care were able to know their heritage. Black families were seen as being able to offer the tools and techniques not only to know one's culture, but also to prepare children for what was seen to be inevitable racism. During this period mixed race children did not exist as a distinct group and were classified as black. The perception that Stealth lacks cultural knowledge is a familiar trope in understanding mixed race and is in contention with the ideology that his ethnic heritage assumes that he ought to have that cultural know-how. These assumptions also rely on skin colour to show us not only where we belong, but also how we demonstrate that belonging. Placing mixed race children in foster families seen to be able to transmit a more authentic ethnic heritage through the transmission of cultural knowledge can underpin placement matching in order to culturally engineer appropriate belonging.

> An ethnic group is a selection within a larger society having real or putative common ancestry, memories of a shared past, and a cultural focus on one or more symbolic elements which define the group's identity such as kinship, religion, language, shared territory, nationality or physical appearance. Members of an ethnic group are conscious of belonging to that group. (Bulmer 1986: 54)

Bulmer's definition allows for a fluid sense of identity that changes and shifts over time and space whilst common sense, dominant understandings of ethnicity and culture as fixed/temporal do not allow space for shifts or changes—ethnicity becomes deterministic and fixed. There is 'no one definition of ethnicity that is universally accepted' (Song 2003: 6). Ethnicity, in this sense, is an emphasis on the group's beliefs—the social meanings its members attach to a shared ethnicity—as Song (2003: 7) reiterates: 'It is a group's belief in its common ancestry and its members' perception and self-consciousness that they constitute a group which matter, and not any evidence of their cultural distinctiveness as a group'. Bulmer further states that ethnicity is more inclusive than race as it is predicated on biological membership of a specific group while the boundaries of ethnicity are more fluid (cited in Song 2003: 10).

Stealth's sense of belonging, when talking of food, demonstrates his awareness of sitting on the margins of Jamaican culture. He enjoys learning and so applies himself to integrating the stories he hears about his unfamiliar Jamaican heritage. His awareness of belonging to an ethnic group is a learning process beginning during his care admission when assumptions and decisions about where he *ought* to belong culturally and ethnically reveal his level of awareness and knowledge. Stealth demonstrates the fluidity of ethnicity and culture and how Children's Social Care discourses surrounding his cultural and ethnic needs are an additional complex factor in finding an appropriate placement.

Public and Private Belonging

Fiona	So, you think that Stealth doesn't like that other people see him as black?
Sheila	And the reality is that people do. Society would, you know the reality is, yes, you're dual, in the fact that Stealth is three quarters, as such.
Fiona	So multiple heritage?
Sheila	I don't know.

Being mixed race often relies on the perception of others to assign belonging, and racial markers can be ambiguous and subject to misrecognition, leading to concerns over classification, labelling, and identification practices. A lack of clear definition over the construction of mixedness leads to uncertain and shifting boundaries for how Stealth's foster carer, Sheila, understands his classification. Sheila insists that society would 'see' Stealth as black and so in order to achieve a recognizable identity he ought to label himself black. Sheila stumbles through language and highlights the continuing reliance on fractional approaches to assign racial belonging, suggesting Stealth is biologically 'three-quarters' and, therefore, so close to black that he ought to position himself, socially and politically, as black. Assigning race to others is often how identification practices become part of identity. It seems, for Stealth, that his foster carer's encouragement of an homogenous black classification has its basis in how she and others see him, and in order to mitigate damage from further questioning it's easier for him to fit into the existing dominant racial category. Sheila's age, ethnic heritage, and cultural location engage with enduring assumptions about mixedness within Children's Social Care, which are a legacy of the work surrounding appropriate cultural socialization as part of a racialization project to ensure black and mixed children know their ethnic heritage through cultural practices. Sheila's concern is that Stealth will experience inevitable questioning over his classification if he does not conform to how others see and position him.

Sheila demonstrates an additional aspect of the foster care system, an awareness of the public/private split and the usefulness of private identities that do not confer social recognition and which generate concern over 'How meaningful is such an identity if it is not recognized or legitimated in social interactions with others' (Song 2003: 60). Straddling more contemporary discursive constructions of mixedness (dual heritage) and simultaneously claiming an out-dated heritage (three-quarter caste) demonstrates the contestable terrain of terminology. Foster care is a space in which wider public ideas of mixedness as problematic, ambiguous, and contestable reveal the private sphere of the foster family as a site in which adolescent exploration of identification is contested by larger macro-processes of care.

This is in contrast to existing research by Wilson (1987) and Tizard and Phoenix (1993) who claim that mixed children often identify as mixed at home and black in public spaces and the public/private split is apparent. The setting of the mixed race family is a site where difference is ordinary and where parents do not share racial characteristics of skin colour, hair texture, and eye colour with their children, and where siblings may not look alike. Home, then, becomes that place where difference is ordinary and children find their own strategies to reconcile identity, to work out belonging, and to choose identification in keeping with how they perceive their place in the world. The heterogeneous family can nurture a sense of discovery in which children are their own racial compass, as parents are on unfamiliar territory in understanding or sharing their experiences and choices. While these negotiations of public/private identities are feasible in the birth family they are not available in foster care.

Care is a public institution which operates within a framework of bureaucracy with systems and procedures which create and maintain hierarchical power relations and reflect socio-political trends and discourses. The macro-structures of care filter into staff training, equipping them in managing, nurturing, and supporting children and young people. The foster home is a private aspect of these regulations, policy, and guidelines which standardize care and which assert authority over foster homes. Expectations of foster care are to reflect public care discourse and policy and to coerce young people in engaging with current discursive constructions of race, mixedness, racialization, and identification in ways that children in birth families do not. There is no private sphere in foster care, and mixed race children who experience adolescence, during which identification practices come to the fore, become entangled in tense debates over how to define their heritage and in which ways it is permissible to express it.

Apples and Blackcurrants

Fiona	So, how would you describe yourself?
Stealth	What, my colour?
Fiona	Yeah.
Stealth	I would say I'm three quarters black and a quarter white.
Fiona	So, when you say you're three quarters black and a quarter white, does that mean you're mixed race?
Stealth	I think it means mixed race, you know. Can I tell you why?
Fiona	Yeah.
Stealth	In school there's a really dark, dark Stealth and they say he's blik. There's two Stealth's in my class. There's blik Stealth and mixed race Stealth and they call me mixed race Stealth. That makes me think I'm mixed race, even though I'm not mixed race. I think, like, in my paper, where it says about me, my profile, it says I'm mixed race. Sheila makes up rubbish. She says how Barack Obama is black and Lewis Hamilton is black when they're mixed race. It's like begging it, begging to be black when you're not really black; you're half white and half black.
Fiona	Or even like you, with a white grandmother.

Stealth	Okay, you got an apple and blackcurrant smoothie. If it was all apple, it would be apple smoothie. If it was all blackcurrant, it would be blackcurrant smoothie.
Fiona	Good point.
Stealth	Sheila keeps saying I'm mixed race when I'm quarter white, three quarter caste. That's what you call it: three quarter caste. If Barack was a criminal who killed a thousand people I bet she would be saying he was mixed race then.

Among Stealth's peers at school, his racial classification is made certain by the presence of another Stealth with darker skin. The young people in his class use the term 'blik' as a descriptor of racial classification. 'Blik', meaning dark skin, is in common use among young people and is a derogatory term that reveals the continuing presence of skin occupying a sliding signifier of value. Obama and Hamilton signal mixedness (and light skin) as part of a new and growing classification to which there is a tangible presence which valorizes mixed heritage (Dewan 2008). By presenting mixedness as the best of worlds, a harmonious symbol of integration and an ability to cross a biracial world, the re-emergence of skin colourism re-invokes light skin as a pre-requisite in gaining greater success, status, and privilege. Stealth is aware of constructions of mixedness in which he remains, as he claims, 'three-quarter caste'. The slippage of race becomes apparent as he refers to the various ways his classification, belonging, and identification are seen among school friends, popular culture, foster care, and social work, all spheres being at odds with his sense of belonging. The representation of his specific heritage 'three-quarter caste' reverts to essentialist language and casts race back to the body. The multiple discourses in use locate and overlap spheres of historical underpinnings, popular social life, and Children's Social Care. Stealth invokes all of these to inform him of the choices that are available to describe his specific heritage. Stealth is beginning to make meaning from discursive repertoires and practices of race-making, finding that his lived experience of identification is not socially recognizable and the impact of public constructions of race cuts across spheres of his private life to question his choices. The private sanctuary of home is unavailable. His negotiation process casts him into a marginal social, political, and personal position in which the public discourses and language of race coerce his available choices.

How Stealth understands the repertoires of race available suggests that he is uncomfortable claiming to be black or to be mixed and outlines the challenges if he were to do so. The very thing Sheila advocates, 'a black' identification, is one that he feels his peers may challenge. This is a generational shift and young people are now more aware of mixedness and the subtlety of skin colour to assign heritage and belonging than previous discourse in which the 'one-drop rule' was applicable. Stealth positions himself outside of the mixed and black classifications in relation to his racial identification processes of meaning-making and asserts his only authentic and known available choice. Stealth's slide towards biological and fractional approaches to his classification demonstrates the need for greater attention to other types of mixing as the population develops into increasingly complex and multiple heritages. 'Mixed race adolescents experience isolation at school as peer groups form around race ethnicity and culture' (Morley and Street 2014: 66).

Legitimate Labelling

Labelling is known to impact on how people understand their position through commonly acceptable behaviour and norms. Stealth is able to isolate and make meaning from 'tracing the history of the signifier, a label, but also the history of its effects' (Appiah 2000: 607). Stealth knows who belongs in the mixed category, as he understands it to mean black and white in equal measure, like Obama and Hamilton. He feels that to claim a black classification relies on being *pure* black and not part white (the knowledge of the one-drop law) and that the impact of claiming black as a classification would deny his white grandmother, who is a primary caregiver and, further, that his peers would fail to recognize him as black.

> Where racialised groups come to promote or accept their constructed differences as distinct and even absolute, there is no legitimate social space accorded to mixed race. (Olumide 2002: 181)

Racial labelling has an impact on the social and psychological life of the individual in two ways (Appiah 2000). Firstly, people experience a process of identification, that is, they shape their lives according to the labels available to them. So follows the expectation to behave in particular ways given their racial identification and therefore to act under descriptions. This is apparent in how Stealth conveys Sheila's expectations of mixedness as an inherently dysfunctional identification—labels portray a certain type of person. The performance conforms to the label. Sheila's assumptions about the mixed classification do not apply to Obama and Hamilton, who, in her mind, occupy socio-politically black identification. Identification is often at odds with the labels that people choose to ascribe to, and thus 'there can be a gap between what a person ascriptively is and the racial identity he performs it is this gap that makes passing possible' (Appiah 2000: 609). Secondly, labels leave very little choice open to the individual and, although not always conscious of acting under description, their performance is subject to misrecognition by others. Stealth is able to exercise choice in deciding how to centralize his identity and what aspect of it he chooses to emphasize, which is fraught with contradictions. His choices are made complex through the psychologizing tendency that casts mixedness as inherently problematic, which is more widely in circulation than more contemporary ideas of mixed race—just as limiting but inherently more liberating—in ways that do not fit how he understands his own racial classification. All of which suggests that he is only able to make choices from those classifications and/or labels that are both socially recognizable and legitimate. Stealth is aware that a category exists in a biological racial schema. He describes himself as three quarter caste. He demonstrates his acknowledgement that within and among the groups that define him his choice of 'three quarter caste' remains marginal in relation to how others may see him. His integrity is intact, as he chooses not to act out of description. Resting in the mixed race classification at school, where he is positioned by default of skin colour, is acceptable but a move into the 'black' classification would induce peer pressure and expectations of a cultural performance which, given his experience of Jamaican culture, he is unable to demonstrate. The position he finally chooses to occupy conveys his understanding of his racial classification, visual appearance, ethnic heritage, and cultural practices and is seen to fit into an existing discourse.

The new mixed race paradigm casts Obama and Hamilton within a vision of mixedness at odds with pathological assumptions of what a mixed race identification conveys—confusion, marginal status, and issues of belonging—into the new world where brown skin equals success through privilege. The illusion of status and success denies the very real disadvantage and identification issues present in young lives that intersect with class, gender, poverty, and geographical location. Such contrasts mark the gap between the varying constructions of mixedness present for the majority of ordinary people for whom leading the free world and exceptional driving skills are elusive. The range and extremities present within theories of mixedness are no easy resting place in which the resolution of disadvantage is achievable with light skin and white heritage—everyday experiences of young people in foster care suggest otherwise and point towards the intersection of other factors that determine their adverse care experiences.

Stealth's care admission positions him within the matrix of classifications in use in the Children's Social Care system and makes him subject to discursive constructions of race-making during his initial care admission. The practices of racialization in situ reveal that ethnicity, cultural assumptions, and visual appearance underpin the ways in which mixedness defines and informs a suitable foster placement. Stealth's narrative of classification considers the influence of cultural practices, ethnic heritage, and visual appearance in the construction of his identity, underpinning his choices as he positions himself through misrecognition and ambiguous terminology. Stealth demonstrates his autonomy through these choices using cultural understandings of mixedness.

The three key findings within the first section of this chapter are: Firstly, placement planning that considers primary socialization within cultural practices in mixed race birth families can lead to more effective foster care matching than strict adherence to racial and ethnic boundaries that seek to culturally engineer belonging through appropriate foster carers. Secondly, the private sphere of the foster family ought to remain a sanctuary in which young people may engage with and work with their identifications with minimal input from the care system and its administrators. Thirdly and finally, engaging with the mixed classification is achievable through its recognition as a lived experience in which mixed children and young people have much to share.

Finding the Ordinary in Care Processes

The second part of this chapter takes the theme of the ordinary and the everyday to examine how Stealth's experience of foster care prompts a consideration of the limits and obligations of care processes and his capacity to maintain an engagement in his ordinary, everyday life. This exploration was brought about through a seemingly random incident several months into the interview process. Stealth wants to visit Greenwich Park, a place he used to go to with his mum that holds special memories for him. He asks Sheila for an available date. Sheila manages Stealth's diary for the varying processes that foster care requires. Managing and regulating children in care entails structuring times for meetings, reviews, counselling—and researchers! Sheila looks through the A5 black diary and suggests that the half-term holiday is not a good week for appointments by reading his commitments for half term.

Monday—Meeting with social worker to discuss review meeting
Tuesday—Contact afternoon with grandparents
Wednesday—Counselling session with Children and Adolescent Mental
    Health Service (CAMHS)
Thursday—Review Meeting
Friday—No plans—but Stealth has exams the following week when he
    returns to school so he would have to fit in revision in his free time
Saturday—Contact with Mum

Stealth's response is a barrage of objections. 'Why do I have to do all that stuff? I want to go to Greenwich Park. I won't have any time to see my friends. It's not fair. Can I go out after review?' The questions continue until he eventually exhausts suggestions and resigns himself to the week ahead. I ask if half term is usually taken up with so many official meetings. Sheila replies, 'Yes', that children and young people do not need to miss school, so half term is seen as a good opportunity to arrange care obligations. Increasingly upset, Stealth throws himself down onto the floor and bangs his fists when he realizes she will not relent. Stealth crouches on the floor pleading and cajoling but Sheila is immovable.

Field Diary 12/07/2009 These small things have an impact on everyday life— what does he tell his friends he did over half term? And then, I am adding to the professional intervention. I'm sure there are other things he wants to do other than go to the park with me on his day off.

Children's contributions to care processes are born out of a desire to ensure their views are taken seriously. Stealth's participation is actively sought as a means of ensuring his opinions are heard, leading to a paradox in which they are in such demand that the commitment to improving care processes overshadows his life. Stealth's involvement in the evaluation of the care system is at the heart of other consultation processes in which children and young people can offer feedback to make improvements. These changes can be outside of the young person's needs. The consultations often fail to recognize their impact on the time and attention of young people, demanding ever more reflective responses and, in this instance, limiting free time. How Stealth experiences his life is split between the demands of care and the desires and interests he is developing in attempts to create a life. The demands of the professional 'team around the child' assert consultation and evaluation of the care system as an essential aspect of good practice and, of course, they set out to make improvements to the system of which Stealth is a part. However, it would be useful to reflect on how this squeezes young people's opportunities and interests to the periphery.

Care Plans and Reviews set out to assure the child's quality of care is consistent, and that future considerations or changes are in place to safeguard young people's health, education, emotional well-being, and safety. The Care Plan considers Stealth's current and future developmental needs, considers how the current placement meets those needs, and is subject to a continual process of reviews. His social worker and assigned Independent Reviewing Officer are key professionals who bring together others to ensure he progresses towards his outcomes—the *future* well-being of the child is at the centre of care planning; the *present* needs of the child remain on the periphery. People who may impact his life are: carers, parents, GP and/or other health care professionals, local authority representatives, teachers, and an independent visitor (which he does not have). There is an expectation that he attends and that prior to any meetings his wishes are taken into consideration and these requirements are in HM Government Children Act 1989. Children's contributions to care planning and reviews were hard won after a series of consultations held with groups of children in care during the 1980s (Who Cares, First Key, Black and In Care). Not all young people are so curious or find such meetings interesting or stimulating, especially if they have been in care a long time, if they see meetings where nothing changes, or if they are unable to articulate their feelings, more so if they disagree with decisions being made about their lives.

Stealth remains on the floor and seems unable to physically stand up for himself and I step in and respond to Sheila by acknowledging that his week is not very child-centred and Stealth is obviously unhappy about so much intervention. I am also feeling powerless to affect change. I suggest to Stealth that we can go another day and that he could write a diary of his week. He does this by writing about overcoming his fear of dogs. My annoyance is becoming apparent as I stand witness and, although my question reveals the reason for such a busy diary, I am aware that its time I left. I feel my anger rising as I leave the house. As I get into my car, I bang my head on the roof and burst into tears.

Walkerdine and colleagues (2001) cite similar occurrences in their research encounters, when researchers left the field feeling depressed after an interview or even when interviewees were happy, cheerful, or positive. Further, they state that 'these emotions, experienced as those of the researcher rather than the research subject, can be helpful in pointing to and understanding what might not, indeed cannot, be expressed by the subject' (ibid.: 90). Stealth was on his knees on the floor, pleading, and this expression of anxiety and disappointment was saddening and my response was anger and a feeling of powerlessness.

Caring About Contact

Stealth	On a Tuesday after school, I get on a bus A171 then A124 and, if my granddad is in a good mood, it's all right but if he's in a depressed mood it's bad, you know? He just hates everybody and he only likes it when the visitors are work people. He gets out a lot, but he just finds it boring at home with the telly.
Fiona	What happens on a good day?
Stealth	He'll make me tea happily. He might ask everybody how their day is and he'll read the newspaper. He'll be happy gardening, but if he's in a bad mood he will look at everybody and kiss his teeth. If my Mum shakes or my grandmother says something silly, he'll just find an excuse to swear and say f*** and b**** and c***.
Fiona	How do you know if he's in a good or bad mood?
Stealth	Just see it on his face.
Fiona	What about Sal [grandmother]?
Stealth	Yeah she's always happy. The only time she's not happy is because of my granddad, but she is mostly happy.
Fiona	Are you happy when you go there?
Stealth	Yeah, if my granddad is happy

Field Diary 20/08/2008 Sheila says that often, after contact, Stealth complains that he feels unwell or he comes back looking down and spends time in his room. She regularly takes him to the doctor as he says he has pains in his chest and, even though they reassure him he is healthy, he insists they are real. I am sure he is heartbroken and don't doubt his chest hurts.

Contact refers specifically to time the child spends with their family members and includes letters, emails, and face-to-face meetings. A Contact Plan is part of the overall Care Plan and details the arrangements for each individual child. Stealth feels he is lucky to have regular contact with his family. He gets two buses enabling him to spend Tuesday evening at his grandparents' home, where he sometimes sees his mum until Sheila collects him at about 8.00 p.m. He also visits his mum on Saturday afternoons. His visits to his mum, he says, can be boring as he has nothing to do when he is there. Contact on Tuesday evening clashes with athletics practice. Contact on Saturday clashes with football practice. Despite him wanting to be with his family it coincides with sporting interests. He balances his ordinary adolescent interests with family obligations.

In ordinary family life, the obligations towards parents often take a backseat as the pursuit of hobbies and interests is central and many parents ferry their children from one activity to another. The paradigm of family life that Stealth occupies is the inverse in which family contact takes priority and immovable contact arrangements, to maintain links, inhibit the opportunity to develop his interests and experience a relatively ordinary childhood.

Being Anonymous at School

Government initiatives to improve the educational achievement of children in care have led to the development of the Personal Education Plan (PEP). To increase educational attainment all children in care have a personal one-to-one relationship with an adult at school who works specifically to boost their academic achievement and offer greater access to opportunities for development. However, Stealth is upset about the intrusion into his school day and the lack of privacy he has when 'official' intervention happens on school premises, meetings which he is expected to miss classes to attend. The disruption to his day is not the only issue: the stigma of dealing with official processes casts him as different. The member of school staff responsible for his PEP requests a meeting with him and those circumstances lead to this conversation.

Stealth   She takes the mick. She takes liberties. You know what she does? She takes me out the lesson to talk about PEP [Personal Education Plan]. I don't mind because it's DT and stuff, but you know where she does it?

Fiona   Where?

Stealth	In the middle of the staircase where people are walking up and down and say, 'How's Sheila? How's the placement?' and someone will come down three or four times and say 'I'm sorry'.
Fiona	Does she have an office?
Stealth	But guess what she said? 'I was going to go to the office but it's too long to walk all the way up there'. It's ten metres or something … she's lazy … she doesn't care.
Fiona	That's quite a public place in a school.
Stealth	I wouldn't mind in the dinner hall. Everything gets done there, but, like, so slap in the middle of the staircase. Doh—on the staircase. Nobody will go here.

The relationship between school and the foster child can be one of the most consistent in their lives, and maintaining a consistent relationship with school is seen as a priority during care planning. The role of advisory teacher identifies obstacles and opportunities to learning and liaises with other professionals in the child's life. The government's Every Child Matters initiative offers a framework that includes children and young people in care having access to the same life chances as other children. While these initiatives to monitor educational achievement are laudable, meetings with large numbers of professionals held at school single Stealth out for 'special attention'.

| Fiona | And, when you leave the lesson, do people know why you're going out? |
| Stealth | No, they wouldn't know, but she says it to the teacher. If that happened, I would complain, but I didn't complain about the staircase. I'm only telling you, right now. I didn't tell Sheila. I feel embarrassed. Foster care is very embarrassing. Having people at school walking around with you like it's a big complication with bits of paper. Ah, this is horrible about my school. Year Nine girls, I don't know them really, but I was having my PEP meeting in their classroom, a door with a window in and everyone, about ten people round the table, me sitting there, for everybody to look through the window |

at us. I get rudely interrupted and have them looking at me like this [sneers]. It's not very nice, everybody knowing I'm in care. It's not like winning the Olympics.

Goffman's (1963) contribution to understanding stigma suggests that differentiation and labelling of specific groups confer specific attributes. The procedures Stealth is enduring while committing to regular meetings at school really do mark him out as different. Whether other students know why he is in a meeting on the stairs or in a classroom is irrelevant—he knows, and that internal knowledge creates his subsequent interactions and identity development. His quietly modest and diligent demeanour is a positive presence but, in his school life, full participation is difficult if there is a sense of shame and stigma brought about by being in care, the regular reminders of which are the 'complications' surrounding his education.

> Children and young people in care, and care leavers, have often told us that people sometimes discriminate against people in care, and can have a prejudice against people who are or were in care. Sometimes this is called "careism". (Morgan, R (200) Care and Prejudice Report Ofsted)

Stealth sees care as nothing to be proud of, 'not like winning the Olympics', partly due to the complex processes that manage the minutiae of his everyday life. Such acknowledgement of care as stigmatizing is known to hamper identity development and to reduce access to ordinary experiences, through drawing attention to what is seen as an impoverished childhood and family life. Yet the processes of care, in order to regulate, manage, and measure consistency, further hamper those already living within an inherently stigmatizing system.

All of the participants spoke of being in care as embarrassing or shameful or of keeping it a secret. The young people were reluctant to meet each other. One participant told a friend in school who then told others. Young people spoke of keeping their home life a secret, inventing lies about foster carers being relatives or staying with family as mum was travelling, fantasy playing an important role in maintaining a sense of normality. Social Workers actively encourage young people not to tell new friends at school that they are in foster care. Professionals often let young people know that building trust ensures that if you do tell someone you can be more confident they will not share the information. The dominant image surrounding being in care is that the young person must be inherently unlovable, bad, and unworthy; self-esteem is often low and young people in care work extremely hard at overcoming these feelings to move on with their lives. Adding the many 'complications' of care processes entailing meetings, meetings about meetings, Reviews, Consultations, Contact, PEP, CAMHS ... places young people firmly within a web of bureaucracy which undermines the very efforts they make to maintain the integrity and ordinariness of their lives. Further, the relationship between young people and their foster carers is caught in this web of administrative bureaucracy, making interventions that undermine the carers' true responsibilities towards the young person—loving care and nurturing—more difficult.

Stealth's management or control over care processes is minimal. Despite his opinion being sought, he does not actively resist the regulatory processes, make changes to routines, or refuse to attend school meetings that place him as a complication and undermine his privacy. Voicing his frustrations at the restrictions has yet to be undertaken with any of the official bodies that oversee complaints as he chooses not to share his experiences among those professionals who may be able to make a difference. Why he chooses not to complain, report, or share this information with the many professionals around him is possibly to avoid creating more complications that may undermine the stability of his placement and perhaps to avoid placing his care problems at the forefront of his everyday life.

Fostering in private families is the most common way that children in care are looked after and, although it mimics the setting of 'ordinary' family life, children can lack knowledge of how to use their rights. Living in a foster family can lead to isolation from impartial expert advice or guidance from other young people who have more experience of the care system. There is a local independent advocacy agency that Stealth may contact, but he chooses not to. Stealth's isolation in the foster family and his inability to raise concerns within his team of professionals, despite the consistent intervention and attention his care life requires, highlights how the intrinsic nature of care planning overrides the everyday concerns of young people.

Professional Relationships and Consistency

Stealth   I got through two social workers and then a third one. I had to wait a couple of months until they came along, but that was okay.

Fiona   Chrissie?

Stealth   First there was Joanna, then Derek, and Chrissie.

Fiona   That's three already, in a year and a half. What are you doing getting rid of them?

Stealth   (Laughter) I just say, 'You're fired'. Well, sometimes, it's because of the local authority and sometimes their own personal things. The first one had to go and get her son and the second one the local authority made a mistake and they were supposed to get a different one.

To reframe his circumstances, enabling a more resilient or pragmatic approach, I challenge, 'What have you done to get rid of them?' Hoping he takes up the humour in my question in which I position him as active and able to make meaning. He does see the funny side and laughingly uses the Alan Sugar phrase 'You're fired!' Jokes, humour, and laughter are useful tools to minimize anxiety and lighten conversation. As Freud suggests, a benevolent superego allows a light and comforting type of humour (Freud 1960). Strategies to increase resilience enable Stealth to see himself not just as a passive victim of circumstance, but perhaps a less personal one in which administrative failures and mistakes are not seen as a reflection of his intrinsic worth as a human being. I enjoy and admire his retrieval of power and, knowing that this is a past experience, it is encouraging and uplifting to laugh about it. Importantly, while young people in care often endure such bureaucratic or professional failings, nurturing their capacity to build coping strategies creates greater tools for managing inevitable future incidents and helps them to understand that mistakes do happen.

Stealth has a good relationship with Chrissie, although he does not see her regularly. He knows he can phone her if he needs to and, in some ways, this knowledge comforts him, even if he does not exercise the right to do so. Deference to the administrative and professional structures impacts on trust-building and secure relationships between young people and their social workers. Research shows children in care cite that inconsistency, unreliability, and social workers cancelling appointments make them feel they are a low priority. They want a more 'emotional, empathetic level of interaction' (Connolly et al. 2006: 67). Social workers are under obligation to carry out specific duties, such as Reviews, Care Plans, Personal Education Plans, and attending court to confirm decisions made in care planning. But, as Stealth describes, these obligations are directly responsible for missed appointments and consequently a lack of time to nurture relationships, making it more likely that issues of trust, consistency, and reliability arise and less likely that children will talk to social workers about their concerns. The ideal scenario is that social workers and children in care have enduring and consistent relationships in which trust and relationship-building are the priority. A relationship with one consistently reliable adult can improve the life chances of children in care significantly.

> *Field Diary 12/08/2009 I'm learning that some things are out of my control. I am unable to make any difference to his or anyone else's living circumstances, nor his experiences with social worker or carer. Am disappointed and anxious that conversation is not an intervention that makes any difference beyond his capacity to see things differently.*

Foucault (1991: 291) describes the subordination of practitioners to administrative procedures as a source of conflict and as a feature of the social work profession. The administrative apparatus and professionals who uphold it are ultimately responsible for inhibiting practitioners from offering the highest standards of care by 'refusing resources, niggling regulations and imposing functions of control and repression'. Social workers submit to the demands of bureaucratic practices that contend with delivering high quality care-giving and building meaningful relationships. Sheila, Stealth's foster carer, is both an administrator of care processes and a carer/nurturer. Everyday concerns—food, clothes, school, activities, and managing his care life—are her responsibility. This creates additional tension in their relationship and she bears the brunt of his frustrations.

Fiona	You feel like she complains about you?
Stealth	Yeah, even at school with the other boy and the exclusion meeting, she wanted to complain about stuff and, because the social workers kept cancelling the appointments, she goes, 'Oh, Stealth, there's an advocate line if you want to complain'. Her whole life is complaining.
Fiona	So, she wants you to complain about your social workers being unreliable. Do you want to?
Stealth	No.
Fiona	Do you feel like you need them to come more often?
Stealth	Nah, I'm all right. I can phone them if I want.
Fiona	You've got a number to phone, have you called the number?
Stealth	No.
Fiona	You haven't needed to? But when you're feeling frustrated like this, wouldn't you like a social worker to come more regularly so you can talk things through?
Stealth	Sheila's very argumentative, very argumentative.
Fiona	And you don't like it.
Stealth	She's just….
Fiona	Have you met people like that before, who argue and complain?
Stealth	My granddad.
Fiona	And how do you cope with him? How do you deal with him?
Stealth	Well, when I go, I don't mind.
Fiona	You can put up with it; he's quite a bit older isn't he?
Stealth	If she's like that at this age, I wonder what she'll be like at 50.
Fiona	You will have left care by then.
Stealth	Arguing is the highlight of her day.
Fiona	Does it make you unhappy?
Stealth	Sometimes, I want to come home late on purpose. I don't want to sit down and have a nice argue. She likes to argue.

Fiona   Do you feel you want to leave the placement?

Stealth   I could've done that when they picked me up from school
           and said I was going to go into foster care. I could've run
           away, you know. I should've done that. Too late now unless …
           unless … unless, I saved up £800, buy the van on the corner
           from those hippies—I'm not even joking—and then buy it
           off the internet using my mum's credit card, give her the
           money, and then, I put all my games and stuff in the van and
           put all my cards and papers and all my clothes, put them into
           a bin liner, stick it in the back drive, drive, drive, to my
           grandmother's house, drop it all off and then say 'Let's have
           a discussion. I'm not going back to Sheila's. I'm going back to
           school and if the police come outside, I will jump in my van'.
           They can't catch me, you know. Then, I'll go back to my
           grandmother's, play my x-box, have a nice life, do my home-
           work, get good grades, and then, every time Sheila tries to
           call me on my mobile, I'll block her number.

Fiona   So, if you could choose this placement again, would you
           choose it?

Stealth   It wasn't a choice, you know. I probably would choose it
           because it's so close to places.

Stealth's frustration is palpable during our conversation and his mind
was racing through thoughts and feelings he was previously unable to
articulate. His fixation on the less favourable aspects of Sheila's character
is consistent throughout the conversation despite my attempts to steer it
in new directions. It becomes clear that his frustration at being in foster
care lies at the heart of his feelings about Sheila, alongside his desire to
resume life with his grandparents.

Coping with missed appointments or the cancellation of important meetings creates a point of tension between Stealth and Sheila
in which their different approaches to handling such circumstances
create the basis for his perception of her role as 'administrator' and
not carer. Possibly, the demands for Sheila to administer Stealth's care
life, manage the meetings, and deal with professional failings bring her
own frustrations to the fore. Sheila's role in dealing with professional

disruptions places her in contention with Stealth and creates arguments in their home life—an unnecessary circumstance—in which she urges him to use the advocacy, and he sees this as another instance of her tendency to complain, despite it being solid advice. The increasing requirement for carers to facilitate and manage the systems and procedures which are an intrinsic part of young people's lives in foster care is overshadowing Sheila's role as caregiver, a role that Stealth needs and deserves.

Fiona	Have you said to her you feel that she treats you unfairly?
Stealth	Nah, because she will start an argument.
Fiona	Can your grandparents or Chrissie help—have you told them?
Stealth	No.
Fiona	So, how come you're telling me?
Stealth	Ha ha. I don't know. I can't trust Sheila. She's says I'm sometime-ish. If I didn't buy this, I'd be wearing my underpants right now and she says to me 'You shouldn't really be buying clothes. You should be saving for your games' and, but I said, 'you're not buying stuff that I need'. I'm waiting. I'm waiting. She's like, 'Okay'.
Fiona	She gets money every week for you for clothes and food and things.
Stealth	I know. She probably puts it in the church collection plate or something.
Fiona	So you don't feel she's spending that money on you?
Stealth	No way.
Fiona	Do you get proper food?
Stealth	Yeah, I get a decent meal.
Fiona	And your room a wardrobe and bedding.
Stealth	Yeah, but it's not spent on me clothes-wise. I'm not even going to be nice on the way I say this now, because it's annoying me. She spends my money on cheap Primark church clothes. She don't buy me no casual wear or jeans. She got me jeans once because I needed it for school. She's so tight.
Fiona	Do you know how much money she gets?
Stealth	No, do you?

Fiona   No, but carers are pretty well paid and get different amounts depending on who they foster and their experience.

Stealth   I researched it once and it was £340 a week or something like that. What does she do with it? I bet she's putting it for her own children's future or something.

This further point of tension in their relationship reveals the administrative expectations of carers to manage and control financial resources. Families encourage the autonomy of young people through giving pocket money enabling them to save, offering foundations for future independence, which facilitates the transition from childhood to adulthood. Foster care administration reduces opportunities for Stealth to gain gradual freedom and autonomy by removing simple choices over what he wears. Outcomes-based research suggests that increasing autonomy can be encouraged as much as possible (Stein 1999) due to the age at which young people are expected to leave care: eighteen—young in comparison to birth children who tend to leave during their mid-twenties. Preparation for leaving care could be more in line with how families operate by offering young people the opportunity to develop skills when they demonstrate they are ready as well as acknowledging their desire for responsibility and control over what they are able to manage. Foster care is set up to mimic the model of family life yet professional discourse and regulation mediate much of its ordinary day-to-day rhythms and, as Stealth's narrative demonstrates, create tension in relationships as well as casting carers into the roles of administrators who deal with professional systems and their inevitable failures.

In conclusion, Stealth's narrative reveals how the mixed classification within Children's Social Care impacts on his care admission and his subsequent *choice* of foster placement. The limits of mixed as a classification, when invoking ethnic and racial boundaries to claim belonging, reveal a category that is both internally diverse and ambiguous. Mixed is most easily understood as a lived experience, and one way to understand this is through cultural practices and primary socialization in birth families. Explorations of cultural practices show that ethnic heritage is not always congruent, and assumptions about mixed children lacking culture often seek to culturally engineer belonging through appropriate socialization on foster placements. Stealth's visual appearance, skin colour, mixedness, and ethnic heritage lead to a foster placement which is at odds with his cultural socialization in his birth family thus far.

Stealth's account also demonstrates how the meaning of mixed racial classification varies across specific places such as school, popular culture, and foster care, informing him of his own identification. Stealth actively resists the discursive repertoires of mixedness that his carer, Sheila, offers, the underpinnings of which reveal the influence of Children's Social Care in how young people undertake their identification, denying Stealth the public/private split available in birth families in which identity varies depending on context.

Stealth narrates his experiences by centring care as an administrative and bureaucratic process that regulates every sphere of his life, from the ways in which he is able to experience his racial classification through to what he does with his (free) time, what he eats, and what he wears. Stealth's isolation and uncertainty in how to manage his relationships to the administrators of care is shown through his refusal to seek advice or ask for help. Stealth's carer, Sheila, holds a precarious position as both primary caregiver and administrator for effectively managing care processes, which places points of tension, for the failures of the foster care system, in their relationship. The stigmatizing aspects and 'complications' of care processes impact on Stealth's ordinary life at school. Efforts to prioritize time to offer active encouragement for the development of hobbies and interests must be a priority, seen as enabling the young person to explore their interests and have fun. Care matters and young people's contributions are important only as they relate to the individual life of the child or young person and this ought not to be at the expense of their childhood or adolescence.

References

Appiah, K. A. (1996). Race, culture, identity: Misunderstood connections. In G. B. Peterson (Ed.), *The Tanner lectures on human values XVII* (pp. 51–136). Salt Lake City, UT: University of Utah Press.

Barn, R. (1993). *Black children in the public care system*. London: Batsford.

Bulmer, M. (1986). A controversial census topic: Race and ethnicity in the British Census. *Journal of Official Statistics, 2*(4), 471–480.

Connolly, M., Crichton-Hill, Y., & Ward, T. (2006). *Culture and child protection: Reflexive responses*. London: Jessica Kingsley.

Dewan, I. A. (2008). *Recasting race: Women of mixed heritage in further education*. Stoke on Trent: Trentham Books.

Edwards, R., Ali, S., Caballero, C., & Song, M. (Eds.) (2012). *International perspectives on racial and ethnic mixedness and mixing*. London and New York: Routledge.

Foucault, M. (1991). *The Foucault effect: Studies in governmentality. With two lectures by and an interview with Michel Foucault*. Chicago, IL: University of Chicago Press.

Freud, S. (1960). *Jokes and their relation to the unconscious* (J. Strachey, Trans.). New York: W. W. Norton (Original work published 1905).

Goffman, E. (1990). *Stigma: Notes on the management of spoiled identity* (3rd ed.). London: Penguin Books.

Ifekwunigwe, J. O. (1999). *Scattered belongings*. London: Routledge.

Morley, D., & Street, C. (2014). *Mixed experiences: Growing up mixed race - Mental health and well-being*. London: National Children's Bureau.

Okitikpi, T. (2005). *Working with children of mixed parentage*. Dorset: Russell House.

Olumide, J. (2002). *Raiding the gene pool: The social construction of mixed race*. London: Pluto Press.

Peters. (2012). The one way traffic of children in care. In Deirdre Osborne (Ed.), *Hidden gems* (Vol II: Contemporary Black British Plays). London: Oberon Books.

Song, M. (2003). *Choosing ethnic identity*. Cambridge: Polity Press.

Tizard, B., & Phoenix, A. (1993). *Black White or mixed race: Race and racism in the lives of young people of mixed parentage*. London: Routledge.

Twine, F. (2010). *A White side of Black Britain: Interracial intimacy and racial literacy*. Durham, NC: Duke University Press.

Walkerdine, V., Lucey, H., & Melody, J. (2001). *Growing up girl*. Hampshire: Palgrave.

Wilson, A. (1987). *Mixed race children: A study of identity*. London: Allen and Unwin.

Website

The Children Act 1989. http://www.opsi.gov.uk/acts/acts1989/ukpga_19890041_en_4

6

Family Ties Through the Lens

Jasmine	What breed is that dog anyway?
Fiona	Um looks like a Rottweiler.
Tallulah	How long have we been here for?
Jasmine	Coming up to eight years. That's Tallulah's first birthday.
Fiona	Nice homemade cake—Thomas the Tank Engine. Do you think your mum might have made that?
Jasmine	I don't know, probably.

Jasmine, age fourteen, empties the bulging envelope, spreading the photos across the garden table. Every so often she picks one up to silently inspect it. Tallulah, age twelve, gazes at the images from a distance. Jasmine picks a photograph of a dog. She selects the only non-human in the pile and chooses that one for clarification. Tallulah needs to know how long they have been with Denise, their current long-term foster carer. At that very moment she needs certainty that there was another life before being in foster care. Jasmine continues to organize the photographs and they decide to put the images into the album in chronological order, with baby ones first and moving through the ages. It is progressing reasonably smoothly; they show interest in and enjoy looking at them,

© The Editor(s) (if applicable) and The Author(s) 2016
F. Peters, *Fostering Mixed Race Children*,
DOI 10.1057/978-1-137-54184-0_6

although Tallulah is distracted by the hubbub of family life going on in the kitchen. Jasmine becomes more animated. They are discussing birthday cakes, toys, friends, and relations that Jasmine recalls from memory but vaguely remembers. Tallulah does not remember: she was three when she came into care, and her memories are hazy.

The recollection, or not, of memory creates fissures in the sibling relationship that become more apparent and important. Annette Kuhn (1995) suggests that memory work is driven by two concerns: 'Firstly, the way memory shapes the stories we tell, in the present, about the past —especially stories about our own lives. The second has to do with what it is that makes us remember: the prompts, the pretexts, of memory; the reminders of the past that remain in the present' (1995: 3). Jasmine remembers stories and events from the past, and the emergence of the photographs prompts new ways to think through the variations in childhood experiences of siblings in foster care.

The long-term foster care experiences of Jasmine and Tallulah can be known through their family albums. The first album includes photographs of their birth family, revealing the dissonance of memory, loyalty, and belonging, and its re-emergence confirms the value of the family album for siblings in long-term foster care. The second family album was created by the foster carer over the last nine years. The last album is one sister's attempt at her own set of photographs of everyday moments, which demonstrate the value of the relationship to her foster carer and sense of belonging to home. This range of visual representations and narratives is a useful tool in understanding how siblings create their own set of memories and lives and how different perspectives may be reconciled.

Pen Portraits

I first met sisters Jasmine and Tallulah at a contact visit with their mum Yvette and social worker Marie at the Children's Social Care offices. Yvette is white Scottish and dad Nick is Jamaican. Jasmine says she came into care because her parents were arguing; her father served a prison sentence for grievous bodily harm and assault on her mother. Jasmine's parents have three other children who are all in care; the youngest child is four years old and was adopted at birth. Jasmine has a deep yearning to return home now that she feels she is old enough to look after herself—and to some extent take care of her parents. Jasmine relies on her social worker, Marie, for a consistent relationship and trusts her judgement and advice. Jasmine has a tricky relationship with her younger sister Tallulah and blames favouritism in her previous and current foster families for this.

Tallulah came to the attention of social workers when she was brought into casualty (age ten weeks) with a suspected fracture to the skull. Tallulah says she has no memory of her birth parents before coming into care (age three). She meets them regularly with Jasmine at contact and says she does it for Jasmine's benefit, as she would rather not go. Tallulah is committed to her foster carer and they see her as one of the family.

The foster family are a married couple with two grown-up birth children who live at home; one has a young baby and a boyfriend who lives there. Greg, the foster dad, is uninvolved. I meet the foster family at their detached home and walk up the drive past the two prestige cars on the driveway. Denise has been fostering the girls for over nine years and receives approximately £580 per child per week.

Family photographs when working with children in foster care are a crucial tool that, when used well, enables greater understanding of children's current challenges as well as how siblings vary in both their recollections and current feelings. The potential of the image is to open up persistent emotional themes (attachment, loss, and belonging) in ways that simply talking can fail to do. However, it is not without its complications and pitfalls. Areas that lie dormant or forgotten in conscious everyday life and dealing with difficult past and present experiences which emerge are distressing. However, there is so much of value in exploring the family album; with sensitivity, skill, and training, it encourages a greater understanding of different perspectives.

Jasmine and Tallulah were about to receive some photographs from their mother—a family album of sorts. Marie, the social worker, gave me the originals in an over-stuffed envelope. It is a strange feeling to possess the images of someone else's family life, revealing intimate details of lives to which there is no emotional connection or knowledge. These photographs really had no true owners and yet they represent memories, attachments, and significant events such as a first birthday party or now deceased relatives.

Jasmine and Tallulah's family photographs do not have the status of a family album and the reverence that albums possess. Images are part of the way in which stories of selves are told. Through attention to the particularity of circumstance, narratives emerge about how we once were and people to whom we were once connected. The absence of family snaps re-awakens consciousness and re-presents half-remembered memories that perhaps have undergone distortion over time. The girls were anticipating being reunited with the photos as they had been spoken about for some time and they knew they were about to receive them.

> *Field Diary July 2008 The moment I took the photographs I was plunged into an uncomfortable intimacy, which then became a significant part of the relationship built between the girls and I—an unwanted intruder, a stranger knowing details about their lives that were only half remembered.*

Responding to their re-emergence, the girls took an explicit interest in their present and past circumstances, seeking reasons and justifications for their experiences. Despite being in the same foster home for the majority of their lives the photo album causes a reflection on who they might've been had they stayed with their parents. The absence of the images during their years in care did not locate them in their past family or remind them of why they came to be in foster care. Somehow, their childhood consciousness did not register the rupture of their lives, and they were settled in the everyday existence as it had always been—without reminders of the past, everyday life is taken at face value.

> Snapshots are part of the detailed and concrete existence with which we gain some control over our surroundings and negotiate with the particularity of our circumstances .... they contribute to the present day historical consciousness in which our awareness of ourselves is embedded. (Holland 1991: 10)

The family album creates a distinct tribe whose members share characteristics, culture, traditions and socialization, festivals, customs, ethnicity, and language or visual appearance. Looking through an album full of images of past and present family and friends infuses a sense of belonging in its members, imagining experiences, stories, gossip, and half-remembered truths as well as lies or secrets never spoken into existence. The album passes down the generations to demonstrate how characteristics and habits (can) originate in some genealogical way—often through resemblance. The family album offers a generational connection to grandparents, aunts, and uncles and contains yellow-edged photographs of parents as children, making similarities discernable. In these images of our past we locate ourselves. These photographs remain with the family and form an intrinsic part of a family story of belonging. Experiences that rupture families (perhaps divorce, separation, death of a child or parent, care admission, or ill-health) can signal a breakdown in children's understanding of what, how, and who is now relevant in constituting family. The physical location of this particular homeless family album was an over-stuffed envelope in the drawer of a social worker and then into the hands of a researcher—divested of the photos' emotional significance and undergoing what can only be described as a type of contamination by people with tenuous but significant roles in that family's life.

The judgement of a family as being unable to parent devalues their artefacts and so photographs occupy low status—not the reverence afforded within families who offer safe homes. When children and young people enter care, family albums are not a priority. Children in care are less able to secure their identities and customs through visual narratives of family life. The absence of their family album for over nine years secures a new type of childhood in which Jasmine and Tallulah are subject to reinvention within foster care—adopting the mores and customs of a family deemed more suitable. Their separation from their family album devalues their historical beginnings and gives privilege to a narrative of family life in which their birth-family beginnings are absent and they become part of a new family setting.

Reading the Album

The photographs of Jasmine and Tallulah's birth family demonstrate Yvette's (birth mother) understanding of the significance of their family album, despite the removal of all of her children over the years. These family snaps were conventional in their poses of respectability: smiling faces beaming towards the camera, events such as birthdays, visiting relatives, and new babies are shown. Yvette embeds and gives her two daughters centre stage in the photographs of her intimate life. The collection spans approximately five years, beginning when Tallulah was born and ending when she was about five—when the girls were permanently removed from her care. Jasmine and Tallulah are seeing the photos for the first time. The family photographs offer a partial view of social lives, or as Banks terms them 'tiny mirror fragments' (2001: 79). Such glimpses of family life are small reflections of specific times, places, and people.

Social research uses photographs within three primary themes: (i) 'context of their original production, (ii) subsequent histories of the photographs, (iii) context in which the social researcher deploys the photographs in the course of an interview' (Banks 2001: 80). In the context of working with young people in foster care, difficult feelings surrounding life within their birth families and experiences of neglect or abuse can arise, and these are best met with the approach taken from therapeutic photography. Wheeler (2009: 1) suggests that 'The use of photographs in a therapeutic or personal growth context in educational or social work settings is for self-directed exploration'. Using these family photographs as a revelatory tool was a complex interaction in which the expectation of self-discovery and greater awareness of their circumstances before coming into care reveal significantly different memories and perceptions of past events. Family photographs prompt discussion and create a dialogue in which the sisters experience an opportunity to revisit memories, as well as to think through how their circumstances were a creation of the people in the pictures. The best way of achieving this was 'by creating a discursive space for family members to revise and frame past struggles in the context of the changes that have occurred in their lives' (Twine 2006: 22). Despite the girls not knowing much about the people in the photographs, the selection of images are their family history and the relatives whom their mother wants them to know and remember.

There are a number of photographs of Jasmine and Tallulah with their parents and relatives sitting together on a well-worn sofa in a dark front room. Family respectability is often shown through the proximity, position, and pose of the subjects in the image, huddling close and posing for the camera 'to generate representations of their intimate lives' (Twine 2006: 17). Family photography has its roots in presentations of middle-class respectability, 'image' of which is paramount despite the socio-economic status of the family itself. These representations often conceal what lurks beneath the surface, and only when exploring family stories does the internal narrative emerge.

Once we decide to work with the photographs, we become bound to the physical space of the foster placement. Private photographs and public spaces are incompatible; despite my own intervention as a stranger exploring the intimacy of the family album it is a step too far to do this type of work in the car, McDonalds, or Pizza Hut—the preferred spots for most of the interviews. Consequently, we spend most of those sessions in the garden of the placement family among the hubbub of everyday family life. Denise strolls into the garden and picks up a photograph.

Denise	I remember that one. They were four and six, that's when they first came, and that's you with Chelsea there. That's down the park. They're the ones your mum probably took. That was when they went to Cyrilla, their first foster carer.
Fiona	Really…
Denise	Ah look at that, look at Jasmine, ain't they lovely, They're beautiful babies ain't they? Is that your mum's sister? Look at Jasmine there, you can tell who's who Jasmine can't you? That was their great granddad, Yvette's granddad I think, who used to look after her. Look at their little car they had there. That was Samantha's little boy the same age. What was his name now Jasmine?
Jasmine	Luke.
Denise	That's it Lukas, here you are, that's their great Nan. I'm trying to think if that was the granddad, because I saw him once. I think that's him. That's Yvette's granddad, because that's who brought Yvette up, her Nan and granddad. I don't know what happened to Yvette's mum, their mum's mum, their first Nan. I think she's died anyway, her first mum.
Jasmine	Luke
Denise	Yeah that's it.
Jasmine	She never lived with her.

I pick up on a feeling of resentment from Jasmine that somehow Denise knows more about their family than she does in conscious recollection. Denise fails in her recollection of a name. Jasmine's face becomes tight and strained as she inserts the correct name. Denise begins to spread the photographs out, plucking one out, disrupting their groupings, and pointing out faces she recognizes while discussing the images. She asks rhetorical questions aimed at Jasmine but never waits for an answer.

The history of Jasmine and Tallulah's family history is part of a public discourse surrounding families whose children come into the care system and is known by professional agencies such as hospitals, schools, housing, drug and alcohol rehabilitation services, Children's Social Care, courts, prisons, and the domestic violence units who work with them. Marie, the girls' social worker, has a version of their family life that centres on her professional understanding of how mixed race families become subjects of their specific dysfunction and has its basis in the race, gender, and sexual dynamic of heterosexual relationships. Marie suggests Yvette is too weak and now unable to leave Nick (birth father), and that he is domineering. They both have a long-term drug addiction. The enduring police and Children's Social Care involvement with the family led to charges being brought against Nick (for which he served a prison sentence). While he was in prison, Yvette was re-housed with the intention of raising the children alone, which she was able to do successfully until his release. She had been re-housed locally, and he soon found them. Yvette acknowledges the demands of her relationship with Nick afford no extra time, energy, or emotional capacity to care for the children. They both currently experience poor health. Marie believes that Yvette's preference for Jamaican men leaves her vulnerable to abuse and that her lack of being mothered (she was raised in Scotland by her grandparents) as well as her social class prevent her from having sufficient material resources and support to leave the relationship.

The legacy of research on mixed race relationships errs towards analyses of dysfunctional family type as normative, meaning mixed families have been subject to a somewhat dysfunctional representation or have been entirely ignored (Caballero 2008; Twine 2006). Research that focuses on the nature of race mixing and the gender dynamic of domestic violence in heterosexual relationships can lead to greater intervention for families seen to be at risk.

Images and Memory

Jasmine	Marie said to me I used to be ber [really] horrible to my mum, like to my dad. I'd say to my mum, I'd say to her, go and get that for me or I'll go and get dad. I can't believe I said that. I wouldn't say that though.
Fiona	So Marie said that you said things to your mum to make her do things, and if she didn't do them then you would say I'm going to tell dad. But you don't remember doing that?
Jasmine	I just remember helping her.
Fiona	If you don't remember those things then maybe you didn't do them? It's not your fault. They were the adults, and it's not your fault they couldn't communicate. Adults are supposed to know what they're doing and you were a baby, a little girl. You couldn't make them fight; four year olds don't have that much power or control in a family. Even at your age, you're being told what to do. At four you couldn't have told your mum and dad what to do. You weren't to blame.
Jasmine	If Marie says so it must be true. She's been with me my whole life she wouldn't lie about that.
Fiona	So you think your mum and dad fighting is because of you?
Jasmine	Uh huh.
Fiona	It's never the child's fault. It's just two people who don't know how to communicate.
Jasmine	She's been with me my whole life; she wouldn't lie about that.
Fiona	You have to believe what you remember not what Marie tells you, especially if it means you blame yourself for what happened. Even if Marie says it's true, even if you did do it, you were four! You are not responsible for them fighting and coming into care. That's not your fault. Things that have happened to you are not down to anything you said or did at the age of four. If they were you would be the only one in care, but you're not. Your mum and dad couldn't take care of themselves, and that's why you all came into care. There's lots of young people who grow up in care, lots of young people adopted, and for most of them they've not done anything to

be there, just parents who can't cope or who can't take care of them.

Field Diary July 2008 I feel the work is making a difference. Marie told me that on the last contact the girls asked their mum why they came into care. They had a deep talk and that it's the first time Yvette has been made accountable. Marie feels the family album prompted it. That and a whole load of other stuff!

During the interview Jasmine is slumped on the sofa, avoiding eye contact. She looks defeated by the enormity of knowing/feeling that she was maybe a prime instigator of violence. Her own memories are not sufficient to redeem her. Even though she recognizes her helpfulness towards her mum and does not believe herself to be destructive or manipulative, she believes Marie's story. She resists the re-versioning of events that may bring relief from her burden of guilt and blame. While Marie's version gains credibility, her own self-knowledge lacks evidence. There is no other information or informer to verify that she was helpful or a manipulator. Underpinning her relationship to Marie is consistency. This longevity, her knowledge of the family, and the absence of any other family members give Marie further status. Jasmine's family history offers her an onerous responsibility as the catalyst for change, which means shouldering the responsibility for its consequences despite questioning the validity of the story. Jasmine is unable to gather all the relevant pieces of information about her family story and her care admission, leaving her vulnerable to Marie's version of events.

Watney claims that part of the role of the family album is to offer the family a 'retrospective coherency', a way to gather its chaos or unpredictability, and this narrative function anchors a sense of purpose, either positively or negatively (1991: 29). Family knowledge in all its gritty detail can often remain unknown by ordinary families and is not information to which children are privy because of their position and status. However, the openness of the care system offers these stories in order to explain why children and young people can no longer live at home. Often the details and horrors of these stories are themselves haunting and would not be told in ordinary families so as to protect children from harm. Children in care live within a framework of knowledge production and validity, which minimizes the accuracy of their own memories and asserts those of adult professionals as having greater validity.

Jasmine's version of her role as a four year old mimics that of all children who can manipulate parents to ensure they get their needs met. They do not accept 'no' easily and will often play one parent against the other or treat the refusal of one parent as an opportunity to ask the other—*pester power*. If Jasmine's mother did not give into her demands or requests, Jasmine's four-year-old response would have been to tell or ask her dad. If he had not been a violent man this behaviour would have been unremarkable and without serious repercussions. However, her father is violent and so her harmless behaviour, she believes, results in arguing and fighting between her parents. Jasmine fails to recognize that she was in no way responsible for his violent response to her manipulation nor could she control his violence. Jasmine's narrative of self-blame overplays her power in events, and what is childish behaviour becomes a distortion of character and self-blame brought about through Marie's re-telling of the story.

Stories about the past impact the present: they have value, affect emotions and actions, and become part of a narrative and rightly or wrongly structure how Jasmine thinks of herself. One such strategy to examine her narrative of self-blame could be, as Fook (2007) suggests, to reframe the narrative in ways that can be empowering. Attempting to reframe the story as inaccurate may have been the only way to empower Jasmine to see that her role as a child was not and could not have been responsible for violence.

Field Diary July 2008 Those girls were fine until those photographs turned up, but perhaps under the surface there were issues. I don't know what the circumstances were before I plunged into this. All sorts of issues are coming up.

During an interview with Jasmine, I ask a general question about where her first foster carer lives, as she holds a photograph of her in her hand. I stumble into dangerous territory. She resents this intrusive line of questioning. She is angry and shouts, 'It's not good there.' I assure her that I ask because I have not read her care file and do not know details that are written about her. I tell her I am genuinely sorry if it was a bad experience, and if she refuses to talk about it that is fine.

Fiona   Are there others things you don't want me to ask about or to know? Because I will respect that. It's your private life. It's about you, and you share what you choose.

Jasmine   You've seen the pictures anyway.

Fiona   Do you feel they're private and you don't want me to see them?

Jasmine   You've seen them already anyway.

Fiona   Would you rather I hadn't seen them?

Jasmine   Some of them.

Fiona   Which ones?

Jasmine   Cyrilla (the first carer) ones of my family.

Fiona   So, which ones are you happy for me to see?

Jasmine   Any ones but them.

Fiona   So the ones of Cyrilla and ones of your mum, dad and brother your um…

Jasmine   and my uncles and them.

The family album enables Jasmine to re-create her own perception of family, one that is private and beyond the gaze of strangers. The value of the family album is intact with Jasmine, and she is the rightful owner. Jasmine becomes the new custodian of her family snaps, embracing their historical and personal meaning. Full ownership and control comes through being able to control who sees her album. She is rightly irritable and suggests that I ought not to look at her private life through a lens in order to understand her current circumstances. Williams (1994) reiterates that family albums really are a treasure of not just kinship but in this instance desires—a yearning for birth family and for a privacy that families enjoy as they store their stories, allegiances, and secrets in their albums. 'Photo albums come to individuals who can look after them, the details of the stories are no longer remembered, and they are private and archaic museums of kinship' (1991: 18). Within the visual family museum, the photographs have the potential to offer a new version of the present, in which belonging and personal identity are made possible through resurrecting family connections. Jasmine wants to speak herself into being through family ties, blood, and attachment, and by taking on the responsibility of family album custodian she is re-creating her family history. Those fragile but enduring links of blood, memories, and belonging that create family ties had been broken by her care admission, but they become repairable through this re-enactment of how things could have been.

Dissonance of Sibling Memories

Tallulah chooses not to really participate and positions herself on the periphery, likely because she fails to remember the people or the stories that Jasmine wants to share with her. Tallulah's presence brought tension, and she was reluctant to be part of any conversations. As Knowles insightfully elaborates, 'Antagonism, of course, is a dynamic between researcher and participant, not a problem with the informant' (2006: 394). Knowles makes a valid claim that although the consensual model dominates research it has much to learn from difficult research relationships. Tallulah uses all the diversionary tactics she can think of not to be involved; she takes and makes phone calls, invites friends over, leaves to play with the baby (the granddaughter of the carer), places her music-playing mobile next to the recorder, and makes hand signals signifying her boredom, notably the noose around her neck! Denise says she asks for 'help' to get out of the session. She reminds me that not all 'research ethics' live at all times in a desire for professionalism. It is frustrating and I become happy to dismiss Tallulah altogether, inventing my own reasons for her behaviour: her adolescent mood, her refusal to see herself as in care, or her sense of belonging to the foster family. Knowles argues that 'handling your baggage in the field' means being aware that antagonism and difficult relationships can be of value. I knew from Jasmine's reaction to my intrusion in her family album that I am seen as 'an interfering do-gooder' without a clear role beyond my own research remit. Being unable to undo who I am and why I am there, I look elsewhere to explain her reluctance. I become aware of the subtle coercion she is experiencing. I ask Tallulah whether she prefers not to participate, and she replies, 'my sister wants me to'. Her social worker Marie also has influence and tells her the 'project will be good for you'. Her feelings of coercion make her continue to participate in the project, albeit not wholeheartedly but enough to satisfy her obligations. The coercion is a significant aspect of Tallulah's experience, and I begin to pay closer attention to the interactions and talk between the sisters, foster carers, birth family, and social worker. This leads to greater focus on the importance of these relationships, and it is the relationships in this instance that ultimately 'yield more rigorous field work, with more insightful results' (Knowles: 393). We are sitting in the garden for the second time one afternoon and it becomes apparent that Denise is influential in Tallulah's reluctance to participate in putting her family album back together.

Tallulah's relationship to her foster family requires specific demands and expectations. She maintains her position within the foster family, the only family she has really ever known, through loyalty; aligning, showing interest, remembering, or desiring knowledge of her birth family possibly undermines her security and stability in the foster family. The family album is a remnant of the past and creates tension.

Denise   Get out there now. Do you need Tallulah out there Fiona?
Fiona   Does she want to?
Denise   She doesn't want to do nothing, I tell you Fiona. Come on Tallulah. Now stop it; you're supposed to join in, and Jasmine is taking part. Lauren is going to have her bath now.
Denise   Yeah, you all right Jasmine? You hungry?
Jasmine Don't look at me, yeah. I've done loads; she hasn't done shit. She can do it.
Denise   Don't say that when its recording Jasmine. That's not very nice. Where you going to have your bath Lauren? She has it out here on the table. Are you going to clear it now? Are you going to be long Fiona?

The younger sister Tallulah refuses to remember their past and demonstrates no desire to tell herself into existence from a family history that has fallen apart and has failed to care for her. Tallulah chooses to align herself with the foster family she lives within and in which she can locate her childhood memory. The unknown faces of people in the images prompt no recollection of who she once may have been within this birth family.

> Family photographs are supposed to show not so much that we were once there, as how we once were: to evoke memories which might have little or nothing to do with what is actually in the picture. (Kuhn 1991: 18)

The girls look at each other and sneer 'What? What? What?' in a way that sisters can argue without even speaking or contextualizing what the argument is about—only they know. Jasmine claims, 'She doesn't remember nothing, so it's like I'm on my own anyway.' Jasmine attempts to make and re-make her family without her sister's memory to validate her story, and Tallulah serves as a reminder that 'photographs may be sites of conflict as memories are our own and not shared' (Kuhn 1991: 21). Jasmine's attempts to force Tallulah's memories to be in line with her own are revealing ruptures and are impacting their relationship. Marie tells me that Tallulah is angry that her mum put her into care because of 'that piece of shit' (her father) and refuses to accept she could make that choice. Their conflicting feelings impact their attachment to their foster family and their loyalty to their birth families—they could not be more different in their present understanding of who they are and where they feel they belong. Tallulah may not recall, as she was possibly too young to remember, but she knows the circumstances of her care admission well.

Tallulah's connection to her birth family exposes her strong and important attachment to Denise and the story she wants to tell about her own life. I suggest to Tallulah that she can take some photographs of people and places that are important to her, leaving her free to embrace the here and now and not be subject to the coercion of aligning her memory with Jasmine's.

Field Diary July 2008 Denise thinks this is inconvenient and that she can avoid the pain of the past by ignoring Tallulah's emotional life. It does interrupt the flow of everyday life of food and bath time, which can happen as long as emotionally sensitive content and history can be cleared up too. She is clearly trying to get rid of this hornet's nest that has landed on her.

Imaging the Present

Tallulah's enthusiasm produces a set of photographs that are intimate. The family members are in close-up: Denise and Greg her foster dad, Denise's granddaughter Lauren, and her sister Jasmine. She took images of the television, the computer, and the food cupboard where all the sweet treats are kept, the cat next door and the front door of the house, from the outside. Tallulah's photographs, in contrast with the images made by other participants, show her sense of belonging to the people and home. All the images are of smiling faces and the subjects' gazes upon her as a photographer are welcoming; no one spurns the camera's gaze. Tallulah appears to be fully part of the family. She is secure enough to take photographs without asking permission. Tallulah is in a very successful placement in which there is love and care and she fits in with the entire family, and this healthy attachment is both right and proper after nine years with Denise and her family.

On the mantelpiece in the back room are an arrangement of studio photographs and the girls appear in one, Denise and her daughter appear in another, and her granddaughter in yet another. Jasmine and Tallulah are part of the history of this family too. The display on the mantelpiece demonstrates who belongs to the family. The symbolic space of the mantelpiece shows those closest to the family's heart. The studio photograph of Jasmine and Tallulah on display was taken on first arrival at Denise's, when they were five and three years old. The integration into their new family underpins and structures how they manage relationships with each other and with their birth family.

Long-Term Fostering and Matching

Denise is a long-term foster carer, but she does not have the parental responsibility given when children have an arrangement for 'Permanency', which is the formal agreement that the carers will provide a long-term and permanent home. The suitability of Denise, as a white foster carer, has been the stumbling block preventing the girls from securing a forever home. Local authority and national guidelines and policy suggest it is more appropriate that the sisters live with an ethnic, cultural, and racial match, if they were to secure a long-term or permanent foster placement. Marie, as their Jamaican social worker, has taken on the responsibility of nurturing their cultural needs (whether or not this is part of her official duty was unclear).[1]

Long-term and permanent fostering arrangements of mixed children in white families is unacceptable according to fostering guidelines and policies, and the aim of same race matching is to offer children cultural knowledge and belonging (Maximé 1993; Small 1986). At one point Marie did identify a mixed carer for both girls but the arrangement fell through. Enduring attention was given to finding a more suitable, and thus more permanent, fostering arrangement. Care planning and reviews sought to identify mixed carers, but the shortage of carers and a willingness to take two siblings with complex needs made it difficult to find a match. During the nine years the girls have been in long-term fostering with Denise, the current arrangement has never been brought to Panel for a permanency assessment. There were indications that several social workers over the years were involved in doing permanency reports for the Review Panel, but none of them saw it through. These delays coupled with a carer shortage offer no choice but for the girls to remain with Denise, who had been initially identified as only suitable for short-term care. In order for the fostering arrangement to take on the characteristics of ordinary family life and offer greater security and stability, foster carers often have greater success creating strong foundations in which children flourish if they have authority over the welfare and well-being of the children, through the rights, duties, powers, and authority which a Parental Responsibility Order offers.[2]

Denise is very keen to get her own collection of family snaps down from the loft. Her insistence that the girls belong to her family too is touching. Denise offers a separate album for each girl. It strikes me

---

[1] She invites them to her family gatherings (but never to her home), cooks Caribbean food with them, and offers knowledge of her expression of Jamaican culture. Marie serves as a cultural custodian, since neither the birth nor foster family has the cultural resources to effectively nurture and socialize them into a desirable mixed race identity—one that acknowledges awareness of aspects of its minority status.

[2] Parental responsibility can be granted to carers through adoption, in which the child becomes one of the family's own children, or special guardianship, which does not sever links to the child's birth family and supports the foster family for up to two years both financially and socially or emotionally through the local authority.

that each separate book often holds identical photographs. It is unusual for a family album to be separate for each child yet contain identical images, which implies that in future there could be a separation of the girls from each other and a separation from their current placement. Are these albums preparing for the girls' departure? The albums include photographs taken over the nine years during holidays (two little girls on summer holiday standing by the poolside in bright sunshine, Christmas presents piled high and the girls in matching outfits with Santa hats in a large, bright front room dwarfed by a huge Christmas tree). The increase in the materialism of the children's lives from birth family to foster family is apparent through attention to the objects in the family homes.

Such symbols of material wealth, such as summer holidays abroad, piles of presents, and the décor of the rooms, all show choices over how the fostering allowance is spent. The material well-being of the family was in evidence throughout the family home and lifestyle. Their means were well beyond that of Denise, who worked part-time as a teaching assistant, and Greg, who drove for a minicab firm. Would this lifestyle be outside of their means if they did not foster Jasmine and Tallulah?

Yearning for Home

During the research Jasmine begins to spiral out of control; she is truanting, staying out late, and every time I arrive at the house there seems to be another boy standing at the end of the street waiting for her. Denise regularly gets calls from the school about Jasmine's persistent truanting, which irritate her as she is worrying more about Jasmine having unsupervised contact with her birth parents. In one conversation, Jasmine begins to confide in me about her relationships with Tallulah and her foster family and her yearning to return home to her birth family.

Jasmine   Yeah, but you don't get it, because since I was born my mum and dad argued. When I was with Cyrilla [the first foster carer], she cared about Tallulah, like in here ... That's why I hate when people go on about Tallulah, like at home, like here. But like at home, I feel like they actually care. It would be better if I didn't

Fiona	have Tallulah. I do love her, but I just don't want to be with her. She doesn't remember nothing, so it's like I'm on my own anyway.
Fiona	*Silence*
Jasmine	Leroy should've been with us still because they've changed.
Fiona	So now they've changed?
Jasmine	They changed now.
	(Denise knocks and comes in)
Denise	Have you finished?
Jasmine	No.
Denise	Emma's going to walk round the doctors, do you want to do that?
Jasmine	Nah.
	(Denise leaves the room)
Jasmine	Yeah, but now I can look after myself, so why can't I move back?
Fiona	That's not a question I can answer. Is that what you want? What do you think you would get there?
Jasmine	I don't care.

Returning to her birth family was not an option, and although they were 'sorting themselves out' they still had numerous problems. Marie felt that Jasmine's return would be to take care of them, as they were both quite ill. Jasmine demonstrates faith in her parents' capacity for change. She offers them forgiveness and redemption through an opportunity to prove they can parent her, if only social services would allow it. Jasmine blames Tallulah for taking all the attention, and she feels that her needs are sidelined and that no one genuinely cares for her. The birth family encourage Jasmine's visits, against the advice of Marie, and this further fuels Jasmine's desire to return permanently.

It is the week before Christmas. We wait at Marie's office for the parents to arrive. It's an opportunity for the girls to have a family meal and receive their Christmas cards containing the obligatory £50 in cash from their parents. The parents are late. While Jasmine goes willingly, Tallulah is more hesitant, and Marie feels that she will give up contact when Jasmine leaves the placement to move into semi-independent accommodation in the next two years.

Marie is using this as an opportunity to tackle the ongoing issue of unsupervised contact between the parents and Jasmine. Marie is unhappy with the contact and suggests that Jasmine's recent poor behaviour at Denise's is a direct outcome of her increasing visits to her birth family. Marie feels the visits are compromising Jasmine's safety and making Marie's position as their social worker untenable—the opinion being that Jasmine is outside of Marie's control. Her managers have been suggesting she no longer work with the girls as she is losing authority. Christmas contact was an opportunity for Marie to propose to the parents that they stop the visits or run the risk of losing the current contact arrangement as well as losing her as their social worker.

We walk through the busy high street towards the Chinese restaurant where we will share lunch. The girls link arms with their mum and almost skip down the street. The relationship Jasmine and Tallulah have with their mother appears warm and loving. Their mum has blonde hair (straw-like from over-dying) and is wearing a black leather jacket, three-quarter-length jeans, and Ugg boots. They look as though they genuinely enjoy each other's company. For many years only Yvette has come to contact meetings, but recently Nick has been coming along too. Nick lags behind. Yvette, noticing his mood, hangs back and walks by his side. Jasmine looks dejected, her face sullen and upset. She is silent. Tallulah links arms with her friend. We arrive and Nick holds the door open for us all. His hair in a neat Afro, and he is wearing a three-piece suit and tie on a warm Wednesday afternoon. He has an air of respectability and hints of masculine gesture as he holds the door open for the women. Does he think we do not know his masculinity has no boundaries? Marie sits with the parents to 'talk' about Jasmine's visits. The girls and I sit together at the other end of the long communal table. Jasmine is refusing to speak. Tallulah chats with her friend. We eat. The parents leave most of their food. Marie refuses to pay for their partially eaten meals. Marie cuts short the contact. The parents have barely exchanged two words with the children and Yvette looks disappointed.

The girls get their Christmas cards, and they open them immediately. They smile and I gather the family for a Christmas snap, feeding into the discourse of family convention reproducing an acceptable and yearned for pose which conceals the chaos of abuse, dysfunction, and sadness. It is the construction of an instant of happiness for them by encouraging them to laugh and gaze at one another, posing them, to display the love beneath the disappointment. All faces turn to the camera. Eyes gaze off in different directions, not the unifying gaze the camera demands of family snaps. Snap. Frozen. The Family.

> Images exist materially in the world, are involved in particular and specific human social relations. Their meanings are historically and socially embedded, told through their internal and external narratives. (Banks 2001: 179)

The images in this family, as with every family, conceal and reveal multiple stories through attention to the 'right' representation, and this has as much to do with the photographer as with the family itself. The external narrative of families suck my gaze into its convention, with a desire to reproduce the fiction of a happy family unit—even recasting and re-creating the dysfunction of this family. Their circumstances are a tragedy, and the desire is to gather the remnants of loss into a conventional pose, giving them the opportunity to fit together, to be as one, to visually reproduce the divisive supervision of contact through a happy image to take home. Through this happy, take-away image, they are able to discard the reality of chaos and dysfunction, not only of the day but also of their lives. Through each new family snap, they can possibly continue to believe in family. And so the image I take is what I wish for their family, or how they could be, if only they were not the people that they are.

The physical image seeps lies and truths, and possibly too much is known about the internal narrative of this family. Their smiling faces appear to mask unhappiness, yearning, and frustration. Smiles are mistaken for grins—grin and bear it. Their body language looks wrong; surely the girls should be seated, cuddled and adored by parents who stand lovingly behind, pushing the children forwards, wanting the image of their likeness put forward first. Their roles appear reversed in the image. In the process of production, the desire was to re-create their family anew. Yet in the translation to the printed image they suffer misrepresentation; they can never truly know how they appear.

There is a physical distance between Tallulah and Nick: they are not touching at all, and she leans heavily on Jasmine and places one arm loosely around the outside of her mum's shoulder. Tallulah is also gripping her card and cash in a large white envelope, which is central in the image. Their eyes gaze in different directions: Tallulah looks at Marie, Yvette gazes off into the distance, Nick has one eye closed in a wink, and Jasmine is smiling so hard her eyes are almost closed. The external narrative could tell the story of any family—smiling girls, physical affection and warmth, the respectable image of family life—but there are clues on the surface, and reading its internal coherency shows this image is one of gathering chaos.

This image fades away and I am left with a memory of the day. There is a long communal table in a cheap Chinese restaurant and a family separated by spare seats and strangers; Yvette and Nick sit side by side, and Marie sits opposite Yvette. Between us there is space enough for another four people to sit giving them privacy and distance. I sit beside Jasmine and opposite Tallulah who sits beside her friend. The communal table is two separate groups, talking, eating, and unaware of what is being said at either side. At the end of the meal, Jasmine is keen to rejoin her parents, while Tallulah remains chatting with her friend. The chaos of the alternative image was the reality of the contact—supervised interaction with their children and being reprimanded for encouraging visits. The dysfunction of the family becomes infantilized by Marie's powerful intervention. Who wants to crystallize that image? A family divided by seats; held apart by strangers; mediating the space of contact, to provide a distraction, assert rules, policy, and regulations. That is the end of Christmas contact. We all leave, the girls stroll ahead, and Marie continues to talk to the parents, berating them for their complicity in Jasmine's visits and warning them of the consequences.

Field Diary 20/07/2008 Today is one of the saddest in the entire research process. It was so full of hope and longing, unrequited love and family fractures— the image of family life both psychically and physically—and it's longing to be real—unfulfilled yet yearned for.

Professional Assumptions of Mixed Families

We leave the restaurant and walk back through the busy high street to Marie's office. En route, I am reminded of the way that class, gender, and race are played out in unremarkable daily conversations and how this is understood through the structuring power of status and place. The experience in the restaurant spills onto the high street. I am keenly aware of power, particularly the power of professional intervention over the lives of families. These interventions are not usually topics of conversational analysis as they take place privately between parents and social workers. The girls walk into the local black hair and beauty shop. The adults wait outside for them. The following, seemingly innocuous, chat begins between Marie and Yvette in which 'mixedness' is subject to a reading surrounding appropriate culture and ethnic belonging through choice of beauty products.

Marie	I took Jasmine out the other day to get her some make-up. She turned up with horrible looking make-up on.
Yvette	Oh yeah.
Marie	I told her that if she was going to wear make-up, then she should wear the right stuff you know.
Yvette	Yeah.
Marie	Forty quid it cost me because I bought 'Fashion Fair'.[3]
Yvette	Uh huh.
Marie	It's really nice on her. Looks right you know. I told her she has to wear make-up for black skin, because she is black. She can't be wearing that other stuff, you know. It makes her look funny.

Marie is an expert whose knowledge, professionalism, and heritage enable her to make a judgement about Jasmine's appearance and what is appropriate. Marie's Jamaican heritage assures Yvette that the embodiment of her experiential knowledge of black skin is superior to any

---

[3] Fashion Fair is make-up for dark skin tones.

contribution Yvette (as a white mother) may make about her daughter's appearance. Marie's assumption confirms Yvette's ignorance of how to instil cultural knowledge in her black daughters. Social work discourse of white mothers being unable to care for mixed children's hair, skin, and cultural needs is prevalent in interventions with mixed families (Banks 1995). Marie reiterates that Jasmine needs her cultural knowledge in an area that she assumes is not met by Yvette, whose nods of agreement seem to confirm Marie's knowledge as superior and her own as inferior. She submits to all decisions. Marie further states that Jasmine is black (through the insistence she use black make-up products), and this returns us to debates about how mixed children are considered in practice and whether they are mixed or black with a white parent (Banks 1995; Prevatt-Goldstein 1999). Marie's professional power to make decisions about contact and make-up is legitimate, and despite perhaps being disagreeable, Yvette nods her assent. Marie has professional status, access to financial resources, and a position of social and cultural capital, and she judges Yvette as lacking appropriate ethnic and racial awareness, class privilege, and economic resources. Yvette's trajectory of whiteness, class, and status in this interaction renders her opinion invalid.

A recent report for the House of Commons Children, School, and Families Committee Looked-after Children states, 'Parents campaigning groups told us that interactions between families and children's services are in many cases, fraught with anxiety, confrontation and a perceived lack of respect' (MacLeod et al. 2008–2009: 28). It suggests that much of the early intervention with mixed families needs further research in order to understand how interactions between families and social workers can be more productive and supportive of families who may be in need or in crisis. One suggestion is that both black and white social workers 'working with women, check their own attitudes towards them and mixed race relationships, just to make sure there are no hidden, counter-transference dynamics' (Banks 2001: 186). Social workers aim to form a partnership with parents in the best-case scenarios, and guidelines enable them to communicate well with families, but inevitably power and status underpin these interactions. Further, assumptions about the parenting ability of white, working-class mothers with mixed children and the legacy of discourses surrounding mixed families within Children's Social Care practice create a theoretical space to examine how such assumptions may or may not lie at the root of the over-representation of mixed race children in care.

> To provide a professional service to "mixed race" parentage, attitudes must change; we must discard our racial myths and beliefs, our racial stereotypes and assumptions about the offspring of interracial sexual intimacy. (Owusu-Bempah 2005: 40)

In the interaction between Marie and Yvette, there was a form of discrimination working to marginalize Yvette's whiteness and class positioning. The assumption that she lacks knowledge about skin tone and suitable make-up places Marie's knowledge as higher status. Research points to whiteness as an ethnicity discernable through normative and hegemonic discourses (Ware and Back 2002) mediated by middle-class values. The privilege whiteness offers remains contingent, and whiteness at the intersection of class and gender varies. In this interaction, Yvette's status as incapable parent (utilizing middle-class standards of parenting), her mixed race children (inadequate knowledge of how to care), her unemployment, and her addiction and involvement with Children's Social Care (part of a growing underclass) position her whiteness as outside of the dominant and normative version of whiteness that affords privilege. This shifting terrain of race-making suggests that white mothers of mixed children lose any status previously afforded and this would have been dependent on class position. White women who enter into mixed relationships experience and witness racism from both black and white people, and they experience all-white groups of people as unwelcoming or hostile towards black and mixed race people (Alibhai-Brown 2001: 189). It is clear that there are dynamics within interactions between Children's Social Care and families that need further research to explore more closely some of the ways in which parents experience intervention—powerless parents are unable to advocate for their children at a most vulnerable time in their lives and practitioners are often unaware of the power they wield through normative values and a professional status which undermine any efforts parents may make.

Uncertainty and Long-Term Fostering

Marie is finally writing the report for the Panel for a 'permanency order' to be put in place to secure the long-term future for Jasmine and Tallulah with Denise. However, in the midst of her preparation she learns that Denise has started a relationship with another man and has left the family home. Jasmine and Tallulah are left behind. Denise confides that she feels she has raised her family (her birth children), and now she wants to focus on her own happiness and build a new life. Denise wants to give up caring for both girls. Several weeks go by with the girls uncertain as to whether they will stay with Denise. Tallulah is devastated by the news and tells Denise, 'I just want to stay with you.' Jasmine challenges Denise about her decision, and they argue so much that Denise feels she is doing the right thing in giving them both up. Marie confirms that the girls are 'emotionally floored', although responding very differently to the news. Marie seeks a new placement for them both. Marie confirms that Jasmine wants to leave the placement. Tallulah wants to stay with Denise. Denise confesses, 'I couldn't do it to Tallulah, she is family. I couldn't let her go in the end.' Marie looks for a placement for Jasmine. The sisters will separate. Denise applies for permanency for Tallulah and the case goes to Panel for a final decision. Denise is worried that leaving the family home and giving up Jasmine may backfire and she may lose Tallulah. Denise helps Jasmine to move out by buying her a new suitcase and things she may need in her new placement. She tells me that she cannot understand why Jasmine is being so horrible towards her. Jasmine moves to a new carer. The Panel consider the case and agree that Tallulah should remain with Denise. In the meantime Tallulah is living at the old family home and cannot move in with Denise and her new partner until he has been cleared through a Criminal Records Bureau. Jasmine gets pregnant shortly after leaving her long-term foster placement.

In conclusion, the re-emergence of the family album offers a powerful tool to connect with feelings of loyalty and belonging and enables knowledge of how siblings negotiate both birth and foster family relationships. The family album reaffirms or denies the importance of biological connections, and despite the physical absence of family their visual representation becomes psychically invoked through memory, experience, and yearning. The greater utilization and value of the family album can explore the everyday lives of children in a deeply therapeutic way as it offers a reconnection to the past, reveals memory in sibling relationships, and in this instance exposes narratives of self-blame.

Jasmine and Tallulah's vulnerability in long-term foster care and denial of permanence was in part due to the endurance of the structuring absence of their mixed family, which was influential in their care trajectory. In this situation the role that whiteness plays is to deny white mothering of mixed race children whether in the birth family or in permanent foster care. Denise, as a white carer, was never good enough for permanence, and hence was on a rolling short-term contractual agreement, which failed to offer the stability and security the sisters needed. After a nine-year commitment to two children most carers would be granted permanency, but the mixed classification of the girls and the white classification of the carer is at odds with current guidelines that seek to place and match children according to race, culture, and ethnicity.

Professional assumptions about mixed race families and white mothering are consistent with the over-representation of mixed children in care. This is one area of research that needs urgent attention as examining assumptions around mixed families can possibly mitigate over-representation of mixed children in care and offer earlier and more appropriate intervention.

References

Alibhai-Brown, Y. (2001). *Mixed feelings*. London: The Women's Press.

Banks, N. (1995). Children of Black mixed parentage and their placement needs. *Fostering and Adoption, 19*(2), 19–24.

Banks, M. (2001). *Visual methods in social research*. London: Sage.

Caballero, C., Edwards, R., & Puthussery, S. (2008). *Parenting 'mixed' children: Negotiating difference and belonging in mixed race, ethnicity and faith families*. London: Joseph Rowntree Foundation.

Fook, J., & Gardner, F. (2007). *Practising critical reflection: A resource handbook*. England: Open University.

Holland, P., & Spence, J. (Eds.) (1991). *Family snaps: The meanings of domestic photography*. London: Virago.

Knowles, C. (2006). Handling your baggage in the field. *International Journal of Social Research Methodology, 9*(5), 393–404.

Kuhn, A. (1991). Unwind the ties that bind. In J. Spence & P. Holland (Eds.), *Family snaps the meaning of domestic photography*. London: Virago.

Kuhn, A. (1995). *Family secrets acts of memory and imagination*. London: Verso.

MacLeod, M., Dillon, M., Scarborough, A., & Tunstill, J. (2008–09). *House of Commons Children, Schools and Families Committee Looked-after Children* (Third Report of Session 2008–09, Vol. I).

Maximé, J. (1993). The importance of racial identity for the psychological well-being of Black children. *Association from Child Psychology and Psychiatry Review and Newsletter, 15*(4), 173–179.

Owusu-Bempah, J. (2005). Mulatto man, half-caste, mixed race: The one-drop rule in professional practice. In T. Okitikpi (Ed.), *Working with children of mixed parentage*. Dorset: Russell House.

Prevatt-Goldstein, B. (1999). Direct work with Black children with one White parent. In R. Barn (Ed.), *Working with Black children and adolescents in need*. London: BAAF.

Small, J. (1986). Transracial placement: Conflict and contradiction. In S. Ahmed, J. Cheetham, & J. Small (Eds.), *Social work with Black children and their families*. London: BAAF.

Twine, F. W. (2006). Visual ethnography and racial theory: Family photographs as archives of interracial intimacies. *Ethnic and Racial Studies, 29*(3), 487–511.

Ware, V., & Back, L. (2002). *Out of Whiteness: Color, politics and culture*. London: University of Chicago Press.

Watney, S. (1991). Ordinary boys. In J. Spence & P. Holland (Eds.), *Family snaps: The meaning of domestic photography*. New York: Random House.

Wheeler, M. (2009). 1992 Dissertation: *Phototherapy - A first attempt to consider the use of photographs in art therapy*. University of Sheffield Library, University of Derby 2009 Workshop Reader.

Williams, V. (1994). *Who's looking at the family*. London: Barbican Art Gallery.

7

A Portrait of Transience Through Care

> And then like yesterday, I heard her on the phone, no this morning, and she goes, "I can tell social services if I want her to be moved and she'll be moved. They'll come straight away." and I'm like "We're not puppets, you know."
>
> (Amma, June: 2008)

Amma has a strong desire to return to people and places from her past, exploring her memories with energy and enthusiasm. Her spontaneous actions and desire to really understand her circumstances are admirable. Her reflections are acutely insightful and she understands why she is in foster care, yet she harbours a strong desire to return home to her birth mother. Like many children in care, Amma does not have a set of family photographs or an album and much of her past relies on memory. She does have a few precious keepsakes which become significant during her exploration. Through capturing numerous images, she produces an album, illustrating the power of the image to tell a story and the impact that the process of production can have, enabling her to have a greater understanding of her life and making connections between her past and present.

Amma's images are useful in exploring notions of belonging to home. She has lived in fifteen varied residential placements so far. The focus on

© The Editor(s) (if applicable) and The Author(s) 2016
F. Peters, *Fostering Mixed Race Children*,
DOI 10.1057/978-1-137-54184-0_7

Amma's needs entails several moves to more experienced or appropriate carers or her desire to be within an environment in which she feels more at *home*. The emphasis on her mixed classification and how this structures her many foster placement decisions demonstrates the myopic focus on issues of mixedness as both a classification and an identity and the appropriate cultural and ethnic match. Amma's narrative forces us to really consider whether matching for race, culture, and ethnicity among mixed race children can contribute to their transience. It suggests that greater understanding of how mixed children incorporate and live their mixed identification alongside their other identifications of gender, ethnic belonging, and previous birth family socialization can inform practitioners as to the best match.

Pen Portrait

Amma, age eleven, was living with a single Jamaican female carer on the outskirts of a large social housing estate. She attends the local comprehensive school. She is the eldest of four children and had been taking care of her brother and two sisters while living with her mum. She has been placed separately for one-to-one care. Amma says her mother 'treated them badly'. At the time of the research project, she had not seen her mum in three years. Amma's mother is white Irish and her father black Ghanaian. She has no contact with her dad and she claims he is unaware that they are all in care. She tells me he thinks they are in Ireland. She had been told by her social worker that this was 'Life Story'[1] (a record of significant people and places in a child's life) work and she embraces the project with enthusiasm. Amma is determined to put the past into perspective and try to understand her circumstances, and she is keen to share her illuminating stories with me.

---

[1] The Foster Care Associates promote its benefits: Life Story work can help children make sense of their past, gain a balanced understanding of their present and, as an ongoing process, plan for a healthy and stable future … a tool to help children connect with significant people and places, their family of origin and their heritage (2004). The time pressures on social workers mean that Life Story is an under-used resource and no work had been done with Amma so far.

Spaces of Belonging

Amma	We're going to take some pictures and that means you!
Pearl	Of me? (Laughing) But I haven't done my hair yet today!
Amma	Okay, what is important to me here? The kitchen, that's important.
Pearl	No, it needs cleaning. Something else.
Amma	My fish is important.
Pearl	But you haven't cleaned the tank.
Amma	It has to be precise.
Fiona	This is real life photography, no preparation needed.
Pearl	Next time—next week—you can clean up and take some pictures.

Amma was enthusiastic about using the digital camera and attended the 'Amazingness'[2] workshop to build her skills and confidence. Amma begins her 'Life Story' project by taking images of her foster home. Amma reveals the important aspects of her placement. These are Pearl, the goldfish, and the kitchen—and she attempts to concretize her belonging with an image that shows she was once here. Pearl's refusal was disappointing but simultaneously revelatory of the rules she places on Amma's belonging and ownership of space. Amma is the 'permission-seeking child' and the 'child in care', a temporary resident without rights over the communal physical space. However, her image production is an intrusion into Pearl's private space of home.

Foster carers undergo rigorous assessment of their personal and home lives to assess their suitability for fostering. Their subsequent approval means they become a focus for monitoring and reviews, which entail an explicit demand for openness and compliance. For example, allowing privates spaces, like fridges and wardrobes, to be checked for sufficient food and clothing for the children they care for. The camera is a challenge to Pearl's private space and she resists its intrusion, as her

---

[2] A one-day photography course run by Anna Hillman who is a local photographer who works with young people. During the workshop Amma took images of the local urban environment, and chose three to discuss among a group of other young people.

participation in Amma's Life Story work is voluntary. There is no compulsion to oblige with her needs or demands. Those factors aside, her refusal enables an interest in how Amma negotiates belonging to the boundaries of her foster placement and how she negotiates the internal space of home.

Domestic photography is an attempt at a visual close-up of an unrehearsed scene in all its daily grime—unwashed hair, dirty fish tanks, and grubby kitchens—in which Pearl was an unwilling subject and gatekeeper. The status of 'home' and its integral role in the ideology of the family is an aspect of Amma's life that she cannot assume. Amma subverts Pearl's refusal to take photographs of her or her home and she decides not to wait until everything is precise. She heads upstairs to her bedroom and takes a few shots in her private space, in which permission does not need to be sought. I wait in the hallway. Pearl sits at the computer in the front room. I look around for evidence that Amma lives here. The hallway is sparsely furnished and no coats or shoes are on show. I look for photographs of Amma in the front room—nothing.

Amma returns to show me half a dozen images of importance in her bedroom. In her study on mixed race children, Ali (2003) encourages her respondents to produce images of home which prove to be relatively unproblematic in terms of permission seeking. The children offer her images of pets, family members, and communal spaces. This contrasts sharply with Amma's experience.

In the relatively free space of her bedroom Amma produces an image with an internal narrative that is symbolic of her disconnection and sense of belonging to her current foster home. The content of the image conveys a sentimental offering of apologetic remorse in the form of an 'I am Sorry' card, a 'Special Daughter' card, and an old class photograph of Amma at nursery school alongside the book *Damaged*—a shrine to her past. These objects on display transcend her care experiences, offering her a sense of self, attachment, belonging, and stability in the absence of birth family and home. The nostalgia sentiment of the image captures the censorship over her communal space and squeezes her into the parameters of her bedroom.

Amma's image and the circumstances of its production show that her sense of belonging to her placement is tenuous; the camera's intrusion was into a yet unspoken area. On the altar, Amma's objects from the past represent home and prompt an examination of how she anchors belonging. Through each placement, each journey, she can take these objects with her; they are significant aspects of her story. The cards are from her mum, the photograph is of her on a contact visit, and the book was bought for her by Pearl; it is a misery memoir about a damaged child. Her exile from the physical space of the placement leads her to privilege her past in ways that assert the importance of birth family and belonging and thus limit the impact of her exclusion in the placement. Such strategies have possibly been born from Amma's transience through care. Amma is finding belonging through the past and relying on her memories to soothe the exclusion she feels at her current and possibly previous placements.

Amma	At least you got me a birthday present. Unlike Aunty Pearl, she only got me a card and I had a birthday party, a barbecue, and all my friends said she was moody because she kept telling me to do chores. Half her family didn't even bring a card. They didn't even know it was my birthday.
Fiona	Was the barbecue your birthday present?
Amma	She said because she spent money on the barbecue and I said, 'I don't mind about the barbecue. I could just have some friends over and have some nibbles.'
Fiona	Yeah.
Amma	And then, she said, 'No, I'll do a barbecue.' We did the barbecue and then she said, 'Sorry Amma.' She didn't even say Happy Birthday on the day. She gave me a card and she said, 'I'll get your present this week,' and she said, 'Oh, did I say this week? I meant next week,' and it's the beginning of next week, but I don't really care. I just want my £45 that my mum sent me—that she said she sent me. Then, I can go buy, um, a digital camera.
Fiona	Um, is that what you want?
Amma	And I want to paint my room. I want to have it stripes.

Fiona   What did you do on your day?

Amma   I went out with Grace[3] on my birthday. Um, I went to church
         and the cinema to watch *The Mummy*, then, Nando's.

*Field Diary 12/08/2008 I feel bad by choosing a book as a gift. She remarked
that there is a girl at school who can read any book—after scanning a few pages.
I wonder if the book is too difficult for her to read? Everyone disappoints her.
She is not feeling loved or valued.*

The family fail to know why there was a celebration and, for her, it confirms her outsider status, despite her having lived at Pearl's for almost a year. Amma mediates her exclusion by relying on her mum to both provide her with some birthday money and to anchor her to a consistent relationship; this is also uncertain as her mum has been unreliable and so may not have left any birthday money at all. After describing her sense of exclusion from Pearls' family, she explains she wants to paint her room, to assert ownership over her space. Amma's circumstances and her image production, given her exclusion from the physical space and her feelings about her belonging and treatment in her foster family during her birthday, raise interest in how she thinks about belonging to home and family in her present circumstances.

Transient Belonging

Amma negotiates placement moves through physical spaces: unknown and unfamiliar cultural practices, racialized locations, and ethnic and class backgrounds. Amma makes sense of her journeys and her transience through the different versions of home she constructs as she traverses residential placements. One way to think through the ideology of home is the concept of diaspora with links to national and familial identities that stem from Gilroy's work on roots, as in where we originate, and routes,

---

[3] Grace is a mentor who Amma has been seeing for a few months. They go out to the gym, restaurants, and the cinema. She feels that Grace is hard to talk to and that she does not understand her, but she likes the trips. Grace is a Jamaican woman who volunteers for 'The Looked After Children and Leaving Care Mentoring Project'. Mentoring for under sixteens is part of a government-funded pilot scheme to provide mentors in order to plug the failure of residential care to offer consistent one-to-one relationships.

as in the journey we take towards identity (1993a, b). Amma has cultural and familial origins or roots, which she uses to explore her mixedness, and she shares these two stories of home through cultural belonging.

Fiona   How old were you when you came into care?

Amma   Seven.

Fiona   And looking after your sisters and brother and taking them into school?

Amma   That's why, when I'm older I want to be a foster carer and I want to have my own kids and treat them nicely, but also I want to be a beautician and go to Africa and go over to Ghana where my dad comes from, because that's a very poor country of, um, Africa and so, I go over there, teach them about beauty because they cut their hair off. I could bring, like, weaves over and wigs so they could, like … try different things. I'll teach them English. First, I need to learn Ghanaian, but in school they don't teach you it! I don't know why they teach French, German, Spanish. I hate Spanish.

Despite her father's absence, she most identifies with his ethnic heritage, as she imagines her future in Ghana, sharing black English cultural practices (weaves and wigs) in exchange for learning the African language, one excluded by the National Curriculum. She can most identify with his race, but not his culture—the symbolic role of blackness embraces her; however, the paternalism of Englishness towards Africa is a strong narrative feature. Her second exploration of belonging through cultural heritage reveals the primary signifier of race as skin colour told through an exploration of her favourite family story.

Amma   She said the story about when I was little and I love the story because I got a birthmark here and, when I was a baby, we went to Ireland and my mum was pregnant with Donna and she was changing me and my granddad saw the birth mark and said 'What's that?' and, because he's Irish, it doesn't clock into his head a bit—because he was old—and so she told him what it is and he goes, 'The child has a disease! Where did she get the disease?'

Fiona   So, your Irish granddad thought you had a disease.

Amma   He probably thought it was cancer because of the way it's shaped. It's like a dinosaur.

Her grandfather sees her birthmark on dark skin and associates it with being disease ridden and Amma suggests, perhaps, he thinks it is cancer, marking her skin as remarkable. The visible difference of mixed children and the reaction of white grandparents can produce strong emotional responses. There are many testimonies in Alibhai-Brown's (2001) book which consider the impact of race mixing on the older generation and how the visual appearance and difference of grandchildren can raise issues of racism and skin colour prejudice.

Amma is a second-generation child of migration with little experience of the homeland. She retains a grasp of diasporic belonging through an imagined future in Ghana and a family story that locates her in an Irish past. Amma uses past and future to anchor herself through familial roots and origins and invokes place as a way to connect herself to the present and give herself a sense of belonging and home—a route, as it were. She uses strategies of belonging through artefacts from the past, stories of her cultural and ethnic heritage which offer her a sense of home and belonging. Such experiences are characteristic of migration narratives in novels such as Sam Selvon's *The Lonely Londoners* (1956) and Andrea Levy's *Small Island* (1995). The migratory journeys of Amma's parents mimic her own transience as she leaves behind family and friends and adapts and tempers her hopefulness to often new, disappointing foster homes.

Amma's narrative of care experiences in relation to movement and transience can also be understood within the political use of the term 'diaspora', which refers most broadly to those who have been forcibly exiled from home and denied return (Unterhalter 2000). Amma is not, strictly speaking, experiencing an exile in the sense of a lost homeland but the concept of belonging through a sense of familial diaspora appeals as it mirrors her own immediate experiences—of a lost home. Amma's removal from her home and family into care is a micro-reflection of exile, denial, and subsequent transience. She uses a narrative strategy to speak of cultural belonging to her birth family, through diaspora, and connections to people, through places and cultures. The strategy of belonging Amma invokes implies she is making meaning from transience as she negotiates belonging through care placements, using ethnic and cultural aspects of her identification in ways that connect her to her immediate family history.

'It is not wrong to go back for that which you have forgotten' (Sankofa)

'I want to show you where I used to live and the school I used to go, to the places that I've been that I can tell stories about.' (Amma (Summer, 2008))

Amma makes a decision to visit her old nursery and primary school—NOW! Her gusto and readiness to approach her life are indications of a positive intervention, one in which she feels able and confident in looking back to her past. As we approach her old nursery school her memories become clear.

Amma	I started school here. It does bring back memories. My brother and sisters, they love London. I remember when they came to London and they said, 'I can't believe it. London. Nothing like home,' and I was laughing. It was so funny because she was like, 'It's good to be home.' I started laughing the way she said it.
Fiona	She misses it…
Amma	It's completely changed. Oh, I know him.

Amma is caught up in the moment as she spots a member of staff she knows. We walk towards the entrance and meet the nursery teacher who also recognizes Amma. The building is empty, apart from him and the cleaner.

Nursery Worker	Amma, I remember you. Do you remember me? How are you getting on? Do you still live with Jane?
Amma	We split up. The place is changed.
Nursery Worker	Do you see each other at all?
Amma	I haven't seen my mum in three years, but we're going to see her this week.
Nursery Worker	How is your mum?

Amma	I don't know but I heard she was doing a campaign in Ghana.
Nursery Worker	Is she? Sorry. Don't mean to be personal. You were in my class, Red Class, which is gone now.
Amma	I've still got a picture from when I was here and I recognize that lady in pink.
Nursery Worker	Come and wander round. Take some photos.
Fiona	That's impressive that you remember the people.
Amma	But it's confusing because I can't remember the rooms. I normally know people's faces, but not their names. I want to take a little couple of pictures just to remind me and, if I show my siblings, they'll know what it is, because we all came here, except for Sara, because she was younger.

One of the treasured objects on her altar is this nursery class photograph, and her memory has perhaps been stilled by time and whether studying the image of this teacher who now stands in front of her gives her a clearer sense of her past as belonging here, possibly stronger than ordinary memory would allow without the image. The value of that particular photograph which occupies her altar has brought her here and confirms the importance of tracking place and belonging through space and time in the printed image. 'Telling stories about the past, our past, is a key moment in the making of our selves' (Kuhn 1995: 2). The objects in the space of the building, such as the climbing frame and the rooms (she notices the changes that have been made), bring back images of the people who were using them. The internal space of the nursery prompts Amma to reflect on her story and why they came into care and how she felt while living at home. She is standing in the playground near the red slide.

Amma	I didn't like the way my mum … The reason why I came into foster care is because my mum abused me and never looked after us and treated us really badly and I had to look after my brother and sisters.
Fiona	And you're the oldest?

Amma	Yeah, I had to look after them, take them to nursery and, then, get to school and then, my mum—I had to go up to the local shop to get her, like, because she liked cheese and onion crisps and she liked mash and ketchup, so, that's why I went into foster care.
Fiona	You did a lot for your family.
Amma	Yeah.
Fiona	Was your mum drinking a lot?
Amma	Yeah, I remember when she left me and she went clubbing with her friends and then she left us and there was vodka and we tried it and didn't like it.
Fiona	Did you used to be hungry sometimes?
Amma	Bin.
Fiona	You had to look in the bin to find something to eat?
Amma	All my siblings know that we had to look in the bin for stuff and it was like when she used to go out she'd leave us there and we'd all sit down on the chairs and talk about a new better family and one of us was always either crying at the end or happy to think of a new, better family.

Amma's care admission narrative reiterates the discourses that guide Children's Social Care intervention and the removal of children who need saving from poor parenting, neglect, and abuse. To separate children from families, to send them away, to regulate and control them, and sometimes remove parental responsibility makes the care system a political site. The determining factor in child removal due to neglect or abuse is often poverty, and families in poor living conditions are most likely to experience the removal of their children. Cohen (1994) claims that 'transclass' placements—that is, the movement of children from poor families to better off families—have always been a characteristic of the care system. The class stratification and ethnic classification of families signifies whether they are more or less likely to be under the scrutiny of intervention. Services aimed at tackling social exclusion through the remedies of assisted nursery places, back-to-work schemes, Sure Start Centres, and health visitors are sites of localized power in spaces close to areas of deprivation and impact on poorer families by highlighting poor parenting. That is not to say that poorer parents are all bad parents or that neglect of children from poorer families should be ignored or even that middle- and upper-class children do not experience abuse or neglect—they certainly do—(Batmanghelidjh 2006) but rather that increasing attention to the standardization of parenting using middle-class values will inevitably result in greater care admissions of poorer children.

Field Diary 20/06/2008 Her spontaneity is great but I worry about her ability to handle the past and my skill at dealing with any fallout. Amma is so determined. It is a messy and complex business, doing research with children in care—unpredictable—and a balance between participation and professionalism is challenging.

Amma's family structure of lone white mother living in social housing and in receipt of benefits with four mixed race children under the age of five years is more likely than any other family type to experience care admission (Barn 1993). White women's experiences as lone parents of mixed children demonstrate high instances of care admission and causal factors of social isolation and poor support networks (Barn and Harman 2006).

Amma satiates her nostalgia at the nursery. She suggests we visit her old primary school. I suggest that another round of questions about the past might be a lot to take on. She replies that she is enjoying the visits, how great it is to get some photos, and that she can't wait to share them at the next contact with her siblings. Being a pushover, I agree that we can drive past the building. Of course, she wants to get out of the car and, before I know it, she is pressing the buzzer at the school gate—like I knew she would! I give her a disapproving look. The deputy head teacher and the meals supervisor greet us warmly. They remember Amma clearly and she begins to field questions about her current circumstances and her family.

Amma   I'm not with my baby sister anymore. She's with my other sister and Carlton is on his own. I'm going to see my birth mum on Saturday. I haven't seen her in three years, and so, I'm going to see her in the contact centre.

Teacher   Is everyone living here now?

Amma	No, Jane and Carlton, um, we moved from the placement where we were over a police situation. Then, we moved onto a lady called Janet and then, my sisters came and then, um, because I needed one-to-one, I went to another placement with my brother. They couldn't give me one-to-one, so I went to my mum who is Pearl now. I find it fun being back in London.
Teacher	Good. It's really nice to see you.
Amma	Can I take a photo?
	(Laughter—they huddle together and smile.)

Amma and her three siblings were placed in a residential home for three weeks while waiting for foster parents. It is known that 49 % of siblings separate when coming into care (http://www.frg.org.uk/, 2015). Foster carers with the skills and space in their homes to take four small children are rare. The size of Amma's family made it difficult to keep them together and they were split up.[4] Since the split, Amma and her siblings see each other sporadically, at contact visits, a complex logistical operation. It entails social workers escorting all of the children to London and back again, meaning contact is not as frequent as she would like it and is decreasing. During the year I spent with her, they had contact only once. Statistics surrounding contact with birth families show that mixed children are more likely to lose contact with their families and siblings than African and Caribbean children. Thoburn and colleagues claim, 'only eighteen per cent of mixed heritage children had any contact with birth family after placement and nine per cent of those had contact with a sibling placed elsewhere … in contrast to the thirty-eight per cent of children with two black parents having contact with birth parents' (2000a, b: 118). The higher instance of separation of mixed children and young people from the ecological benefits of family life signifies that they will experience greater problems as care leavers without family connections to sustain them into adulthood. Mixed young people experience such

---

[4] In recognition of this issue more generally Delma Hughs set up a group called 'Siblings Together' which offers siblings in care, separated through foster placements, a holiday together.

higher rates of disruption and instability that their disadvantages in all areas of concern are markedly greater than for other ethnic groups (Barn et al. 2005). The inconsistency and confusion surrounding what constitutes an appropriate ethnic and racial foster placement for mixed children means they are less likely to experience stability.

What is Transience?

Research evidence on the movement of children through care over the past forty years points to a failure to adequately safeguard children from frequent disruption and placement movement. As early as the 1970s, an empirical study by Stein and Carey claimed the average number of placements was 4.2 per young person in care (1986). During the 1990s, approximately 40% had four or more moves and, within this, 10% moved more than ten times (Biehal et al. 1992; Biehal and Wade 1996). The 2010–2014 trend reveals that 30–40% of all young people in care experience more than four moves and, within this group, 6–10% have over ten moves (Stein 2005). Current statistics from the Department for Education state that 67% experience one placement, 22% experience two placements, and 11% experience three or more placements, statistics unchanged since 2010. A recent survey carried out by the Children's Commissioner for England in the State of the Nation Report: Children in Care and Care Leavers states 39% experience between one and three moves and 10% more than four moves (2015). An earlier survey by the Children's Commissioner stated that 25% of children were not given any notice they were moving. Fifty per cent were given one week's notice (2012).

Amendments to the Children Act 1989 (Para. 1.5) says, 'A change of home, carer, social worker, or school almost always carries some risk to the child's development and welfare.' It would be prudent not to move children once they are settled unless there is just cause for doing so. Matching criteria aside, there appear to be other circumstances which prompt such decisions to be made. Research evidence suggests, '[t]here is concern that children may have been moved predominantly for financial reasons, even where remaining with their IFP (Independent Fostering Provider) would've been in their best interests' (Fayle 2015). There is a widespread belief among local authority departments that private fostering providers are more expensive than in-house local authority options and, in financially stretched departments, social workers are encouraged to select in-house care when it becomes available, even if the child has been settled with an IFP for many years. However, conclusions of the report suggest that more research into the true cost analysis of in-house versus IFP needs undertaking as services extraneous to the carer's allowance are paid for from a separate budget within local authority in-house placements. Greater research into cost analysis could provide more stability for children who move to meet budget constraints of Children's Social Care departments.

> To accurately compare the costs of local authority services and independent services, and improve the understanding of the role cost plays in providing placements that meet the needs of children. (Fayle 2015)

The Fostering Network advocates that good quality placements and appropriate matching are the key characteristics of successful placements, ensuring stability and consistency of care (2004). Findings by Barn and colleagues suggest that 'Local authorities actively seek to avoid disruption and instability to avoid social exclusion and accumulative disadvantage in the lives of young people' (2005: 5). When it is impossible to ethnically match a child to a foster family, there can be assurances that their cultural needs are met in the community. Amma's ability to rise above what are trying circumstances of excessive placement movement reveals that transience is both a causal factor and an effect. The complexity of the lives of children who struggle to make sense of their circumstances and perceptions of their identification needs greater engagement. It is crucial that there be support, resources, and encouragement for foster families to develop the necessary patience to provide stability, particularly for mixed race children, who are more likely to be in care and more likely to be transient.

Matching for Race, Culture, and Ethnic Heritage

Amma   I try and get on with life, like Aunty Pearl, she's really great. I'm not racist or anything, but I was with a lot of white women that, like, couldn't see what I was going through and I wanted to be a part of both of them. I was with too many of them. At the same time, I wanted to be black again, as well. That's why I went to Aunty Pearl.

Fiona   Has she helped you find that part of yourself?

Amma   But Aunty Pearl is Jamaican.

The conflation of race as culture is revealed as Amma asserts that despite Pearl's 'race', that is, her symbolic and political position as black, Pearl's Jamaican cultural practices are at odds with her own Irish and Ghanaian parentage. She expresses her desire to be both black and white; however, in her specific circumstances and in social practice, living as both is problematic due to the wider practices of race-making that determine definition. Amma's both-ness continues to be elusive as she negotiates Pearl's Jamaican expression of culture through church attendance, parenting practices, expectations of behaviour, food preferences, and Amma's responsibilities and chores around the home. Pearl conforms to Jamaican standards of parenting that assert discipline, obedience, and respect and, although these are admirable values, Amma refuses to defer completely to Pearl's ways of doing things as they are oppositional to how she understands aspects of family life. As a black foster carer, Pearl is thought to be able to engage with Amma's 'identity' and also to meet her needs for a warm, significant relationship and one-to-one care. However, subsuming race with ethnicity leads to difficulties over cultural expectations, care, customs, and ethnic and cultural differences.

The conundrum of matching mixed children has a part to play in Amma's placement movement and her ability to fit in with her foster families, contributing to her getting excessive numbers of short-term placements. The foster care system has a shortfall of Black Minority Ethnic (BME) carers who are in demand in local authority areas with high care admission rates of BME children. The Children Act 1989 states that due consideration should be given to 'a child's religious persuasion, racial origin, and cultural and linguistic background' (1989: section 22, 5, c). This policy framework for placement makes a number of considerations to ensure an appropriate match[5] and, in current matching practice for fostering, mixed children can be considered through two competing paradigms. Firstly, the Liberal perspective that asserts loving families of any ethnicity are suitable places to raise black and mixed children and shorten the time they wait in residential children's homes without permanent loving families. The Action Plan on Adoption, led by the Conservative Government in 2012, has cut down waiting times for black, mixed, and Asian children within this Liberal model. Secondly, the black paradigm argues that the Liberal perspective ignores children's culture, heritage, and religion and does not equip them with the skills to live in a world in which race and racism will influence their experiences and opportunities. While these competing perspectives differ in their approach to securing appropriate placements, they both share a desire to consider the overriding social and emotional needs of a child for a stable, secure, and loving family. As yet, there is no formal requirement for fostering placements to invoke the guidelines for adoption in their disregard of race, ethnicity, and culture and it remains a matching criterion in fostering placements.

High demand for fostering placements and a shortage of black and mixed families in the majority of local authorities results in placing children with any available family. Often, children are in an emergency situation, needing a safe place to sleep that night, and it becomes irrelevant

---

[5] Children Act 1989 Guidance and Regulations, Volume 3 Family Placement; and Volume 4 Residential Care. These requirements include:

duty to promote and safeguard the child's welfare
duty to consider the wishes and feelings of the child
duty to consider the wishes and feelings of the parents
duty to consider the child's religious persuasion, racial origin and cultural and linguistic background
duty to make arrangements for the child to live with a parent, someone with parental responsibility, or a relative, friend, or person connected with the child, unless this would be impractical or inadvisable
duty to provide accommodation near a child's home
duty to place siblings together where appropriate

what the ethnic, cultural, or linguistic background of that family might be. However, once a child is in a placement, more suitable alternative placements are sought and children frequently move on, once those placements become available. Despite the recognition that ethnically appropriate matches do not, by themselves, lead to good-quality and consistent care, it remains a factor. It is crucial to challenge the assumption that sharing skin colour leads to good parenting. An over-emphasis on ethnic and racial matching can override more careful attention to the importance of the child's primary socialization and their longer-term emotional and social needs.

The ideal preference for BME carers for mixed children is premised upon the belief that they will be seen as black by society and so they need preparation for inevitable racism. Such carers are then equipped to transmit what is believed to be an authentic and discrete 'black culture,' despite it being contentious as to whether there is such a phenomenon. This undermines the nature and structure of mixed families who, by their very nature, may express and practise more than one culture. Such social and political beliefs negate and undermine the practices and social legitimacy of interracial families who are able to successfully raise mixed children.

The shortage of BME carers impacts mostly on mixed children in care: '84% of all mixed children are placed with white carers, while 55% of children with two BME parents are placed with white carers' (Thoburn et al. 2000a, b: 117). There is a greater emphasis placed on supporting the racial and ethnic identity needs of children in care with two black parents, which confirms the findings of the study by Barn and colleagues (2005) which suggest that black African or Caribbean children experience greater stability. BME foster families are a priority for children who have a greater need for cultural socialization into the culture to which they visibly belong.

However, mixed race children are suitable matches for white carers as this mostly reflects their birth family and primary socialization and attachment. Importantly, these placements are not seen as suitable for longer-term stability or permanence, as shown in Jasmine and Tallulah's long-term fostering experience. Although mixed children are seen as black—because that is how society will see them—they are not a priority for cultural socialization in a BME foster family. Instead, white carer placements more often care for mixed children. If no suitable placement is found, the children stay in what is thought to be unsuitable long-term care or a series of short-term placements, each marginally better than the previous, leading to both transience and insecure long-term placements. Policy guidelines disregard white carers as suitable placements for mixed children, yet the scarcity of BME carers means they do not have priority over those placements which go to children with two black parents who are understood to be needing a BME family more than a mixed child. Therefore, mixed children experience greater instability and transience as they are seen not to belong with white carers long-term, despite this often being a reflection of their birth families.

What is ordinary within mixed family life is denied by Children's Social Care practices and policy. So, for example, the belief that white mothers cannot successfully raise or care for mixed children means that placements with white carers are always spoken of as 'inappropriate'. Part of the problem with this Children's Social Care discourse, which Amma reiterates and acts upon when she asserts, 'I was with a lot of white women that couldn't see what I was going through', is its impact on the young people themselves. These discursive repertoires circulate as explicit reasons for moving mixed young people through a number of short-term white foster carers because they are seen as being unable to do the work of race, that is, preparing children for a racialized world. For Amma, this political position becomes personal and the designation of white carers as poor mother substitutes with an inability to parent confirms her perception of her mother's failure. This position and perception of inadequate white mothering persists, despite their role in successfully parenting mixed children in birth families across Britain over generations.

Locations: Multiracial and Multiethnic Areas

Amma's transience through foster homes highlights how race, ethnicity, culture, and geographical and class boundaries implicitly and explicitly structure her placements. Amma's geographical location of Cambridge, surrounded by people from a different class background and in a predominantly white area, was disastrous for her. She described feeling as though she did not fit in, that she had the wrong class background (Skeggs 1997). Social class and location are crucial to children's sense of belonging and their ability to fit into foster families. Amma says, 'I didn't like Paxton because it was too posh and I'd already been to a private school and it was really … I tried to do suicidal in it, so that's why I didn't like it.' Amma suggests that this experience of not fitting into a predominantly white, middle-class area informed her decision to return to London, her subsequent choice of secondary school, and the knowledge that choice of school is crucial as she claims, 'I like to be myself in school.' Her strong attachment to being herself signals that her belonging in placements could be tenuous as she is possibly unable to be herself and thus she positions school as the place where she is most comfortable. Research findings from Barn and colleagues (2005) suggest that a multiracial locality may help mixed children feel secure in their individual and group ethnic identity and thus promote their resilience and belonging.

Research with mixed families outside of social services intervention points to the importance of a multiethnic area for parents raising mixed families (Caballero et al. 2008). Census data shows that mixed families with children are more likely to live in multicultural metropolitan areas and such clustering may be due to several factors. They may have always lived there, they may have chosen to raise children there because of a diverse population, or they may have felt a multiracial and multiethnic location is an important aspect of raising mixed children (2008: 41). The majority of Amma's placements with white women were outside of the multiethnic area where she grew up.

The rural locations, class backgrounds, ethnicity, and cultures of her carers suggest that many of Amma's placements enable her to step back and decide her own rules about where she most easily fits in and who she is most comfortable with. Amma has to adapt like a chameleon in order to survive in care. There are aspects of her identification that she refuses to relinquish, such as her class background and attachment to London. Mixedness, as a practice of identification, is fluid and shifts in encounters across other axes of similarity and difference as it intersects and interacts with biography, gender, location, and class, making new forms of identification possible. Amma's fostering experiences have led to her sense of dislocation; she traverses boundaries of race, class, culture, and geography, continually moved onto more 'appropriate' placements, and her transience, aside from dislocation, has an additional consequence of risk.

Risks of Foster Care

Amma travels through many foster homes and is vulnerable through her dislocation, isolation, and reduction in social worker contact. Amma's social worker reduces contact because of the physical distance of placements and she sometimes does not see her for months at a time. Amma's isolation (as in Stealth's narrative) results in physical and emotional abuse, which goes undetected because of less social worker contact.

Amma   I call Aunty Pearl 'mum' sometimes, because I forget which one, all the time that I used to call people mum, like Maria. She was a foster carer, but, um, she abused us while we were in foster care and then she got arrested and then we got moved.[6]

Fiona   How long were you with her?

Amma   Eighteen months.

Fiona   What was she doing?

Amma   Hitting us. I remember she had this party and me and my sister— I was crying because I wanted her—because she said she would read us a story and then she didn't, so I was crying and she did that [she holds her hand flat over her mouth] held her hand over my face and I started to bleed and then I was in this room and there was cameras on me and I had to wear this thing here and they interviewed me and she had fostered six children.

Fiona   Had she abused you all?

Amma   Not my baby sister, though—she was her favourite—but Donna got hit with wooden spoons.

The move towards foster homes was partly an outcome of abuse scandals: foster care was thought to minimize the risk of abuse present in large

---

[6] Amma later received criminal compensation as the carer was found guilty of abuse and banned from fostering children.

residential homes. Instances of child abuse and death in the home of the birth family make the headlines when social workers fail to spot the signs. Culpability often lies with the professionals while parents are failed by the system designed to protect them and their children. Child protection procedures and even the removal of children at risk do not mitigate the potential for harm (Ritchie 2005). Once children are admitted into care, there ceases to be any systematic data collation or evaluation of the risk of care, despite abuse in residential care and foster homes being brought to public attention through enquiries into abuse scandals.[7] Recently, numerous reports of sexual abuse highlight the complicit nature of care home staff in allowing sexual predators to abuse children. Global research data on abuse in residential care suggests that 'public care may be a greater risk than remaining in the family' (Ritchie 2005: 3). An American study found that abuse and deaths in foster care appear at three times the frequency of the general population (Nunno and Motz 1988: 3). The Waterhouse (2000) report suggests young people in residential homes and foster care are less likely to report abuse or to have it forwarded to the appropriate authorities. Amma's endurance of abuse at a foster placement, her failure to report it, and the ensuing court case culminating in a criminal compensation award highlight one risk of transience through care.

Transience and Resilience

Amma   Now her fiancé is going to move in and I hate him. He gets too involved.
Fiona   How?
Amma   When Aunty Pearl tells me off, he's getting involved in that.
Fiona   He has an opinion?

---

[7] a. John Darby, who ran the Hollydale Children's Home 1971–1983, was found dead at his home in 2010, just prior to his court appearance on charges including sexual offences and cruelty.
b. In 1971 Edward Paisnel was sentenced to thirty years in Jersey for charges of assault and sexual offences. It is suspected he was linked to the child murders at the Haut de la Garenne home.
c. North Wales has the largest ever enquiry into abuse in homes. Allegations of a council cover-up and a failure to take complaints seriously led to retrospective court cases and compensation awards for hundreds of victims. Some abusers have been jailed.

Amma	And he's going to move in when they get married which is November; they're going to Bahamas.
Fiona	Quite soon isn't it.
Amma	They didn't tell me. I had to find out by myself.
Fiona	How did you find out?
Amma	I listen. I'm not very stupid. I do listen to stuff.
Fiona	Does Pearl know you want to move?
Amma	I think she does, um, suspect it.
Fiona	Um.
Amma	And then, like, yesterday, I heard her on the phone—no this morning—and she goes, 'I can tell social services if I want her to be moved and she'll be moved they'll come straight away,' and I'm like, 'We're not puppets, you know.'

Increasing resilience among children and young people in care is a growing part of social work and practitioner training. The emphasis is put back on the individual to overcome their circumstances. In social work literature, resilience is about overcoming the odds, coping with adverse circumstances, and making a recovery. Resilience and protective factors are the positive side of risk and vulnerability within the child and within the child's environment (Stein 2005). Resilience entails moving away from a focus on the problems of the care system towards a focus on the positive aspects of individual children's lives and how some (but not all) children manage to overcome institutional failings in their care experiences. Some of these protective factors can be difficult to secure if young people experience a transient care life or receive poor quality care. However, a focus on building and relying on the capacity of the young person to build resilience omits an engagement with the very practices that make the concept of resilience a pre-requisite for young people in care. While resilience is an essential life skill, its over-application negates poor practice and burdens children in both foster and residential care with the responsibility for overcoming what can be dire circumstances over which they have little control.

Amma is becoming increasingly distant, appearing worried, tired, and stressed. We are in Greenwich Park, one of her 'historic places'—a place she used to visit with her birth family. She wants to get into the children's playground and go on the swing but insists that the main gate is too far to walk to so she begins to scale the fence. Later on, when returning to the car, she is hesitant about going home. She also has a rash all over her face, is complaining that she was unwell yesterday, she has toothache, and now tells me she has not eaten lunch and it is after five o'clock.

The transience narrative has a powerful hold over her and she begins to convince herself that moving out is the only solution. Amma's exclusion from Pearl's decision-making and not being privy to her wedding plans distresses her. Further, she now feels insecure at the placement as the marriage means inevitable changes. She overhears Pearl's conversation with social services about her being moved and is angry at the power she has to put Amma back into the care system. She resents that she can be moved at short notice without her consent upon the say-so of the carer. Amma has been asking her social worker to be moved for a few weeks and no action has been taken, leaving her upset and angry.

Amma	I'm very bored. Please don't take me home. Don't take me home.
Fiona	Amma, how about talking to Pearl about how you feel?
Amma	She's going to start an argument.
Fiona	What do you argue about?
Amma	I do try and do my chores but sometimes, yeah, I hate it. Like, yesterday, I had to do underneath my bed and everywhere. I had loads of mess and had a migraine, my throat was hurting, and I was hot and sleepy. I told her I need an aspirin and she said, 'Go upstairs Amma.'
Fiona	Were you ill? You have this rash … how long?
Amma	All I want in my whole entire life, if I could have one wish, is to be with my mum.
Fiona	What would you like to say to Pearl to help her understand?
Amma	I don't want to say nothing. She should already understand. That's what foster carers are meant to do, understand.
Fiona	She's human, too Amma.
Amma	I know she thinks everything's normal and it's not. In front of the social worker, she acts all right and she isn't.

Amma and Pearl's focus on chores may be a distraction from the transition they are experiencing; it is safer for Pearl to blame Amma for not doing chores than to meet her insecurity surrounding her impending marriage. Amma tells me, 'I missed out on my childhood because I had to do chores, and now I just hate chores.' Her room, her private space where she can take photographs without censorship, now comes under the supervision of Pearl who insists on certain standards of hygiene. The tension and arguments over an issue common to most teenagers—an untidy bedroom—mask the real threat Amma feels over her immediate future and the arrival of Pearl's new husband. The private space of the foster placement exposes Amma to changes in the personal lives of carers and to adaptations in living arrangements, which threaten her. She has come to Pearl for one-to-one care. Pearl is not allowed to foster any other children while Amma lives there in order to focus on giving Amma the consistent one-to-one relationship that has so far been elusive.

Field Diary 10/09/2008 Amma's situation is spiralling out of control. There appears to be no immediate support. She does not know when she is seeing her new social worker next. I was drawn into making an intervention, which made things worse. Amma has very few ways of making her feelings known.

Eventually, after much cajoling, we arrive back at the placement, but no one is at home. We wait in the car. Pearl arrives. Amma refuses to leave the car. Pearl approaches. She asks if Amma has told me what has been happening. She asks me to come in. Amma wants me to. We all sit in the front room. Pearl and Ezra begin to talk about Amma and the gripes they have which centre on her reluctance to clean her room. They say that she has been moody and uncooperative. I hear them out, all the while thinking that this scenario could be part of any other family's life too, except they appear to be bullying in their manner and are ganging up on her. Ezra, in particular, is verbally aggressive and crossing the boundary of personal privacy as he talks about Amma's hygiene, manners, and character.

Amma sits looking down at the floor. She begins to say that she felt sick yesterday and couldn't do her chores. She says that she does try to clean her room and keep it tidy. They retort that her efforts are not good enough. Amma leaves the room and goes upstairs. They continue to talk at me and by the time I excuse myself moments later and follow Amma upstairs, I hear a loud thudding noise. Her bedroom window is wide open. She has jumped from the first floor.

Moving On

I call later that evening to see if Amma has returned. Pearl says the police are looking for her. They find her later that night at her mum's house, sleeping in a tent in the back garden. Pearl says she is sorry the placement is breaking down and that she has been asking for respite care for months, but is receiving very little support from the social worker as they go from one crisis to the next. I make an arrangement to visit Amma.

Towards the end of the research Amma is having increasing contact with her mum, who wants her back home. They were in touch via email, MSN, and mobile phone—all disallowed by social services. Social workers find it challenging to regulate contact between children and parents with the increase in personal forms of communication and social media.

Field Diary 15/09/2008 Pearl rang to say that I shouldn't come this afternoon as Amma was moving out that evening. Amma's mum rang social services to tell them she was being mistreated. Her mum remains the only consistent figure in her life after all these years of care, she still wants her.

Amma says she is sure she will stay at the same school and area. She seems happy to be moving on. Her new placement is not without complication. She lives with experienced Caribbean foster carers and two sisters, also Caribbean, who have been with the family for several years and are moving towards permanence with them. Amma is sandwiched between the girls in age. The neighbouring local authority and the social worker of the sisters object to Amma's presence in the placement as they argue the three girls are too close in age. The carers insist they can cope with all three girls and Amma seems to be thriving with this experienced foster family. However, the neighbouring local authority issues an ultimatum to the carers: choose which placement to continue with. Amma moves on from the placement to an inexperienced foster carer where she regularly runs away. She has since moved on again, and is now living with another carer, which will probably not be her last.

In conclusion, Amma aims to anchor belonging through taking images at her foster placement and her exclusion leads to nostalgia for her birth family, community, and significant places from the past. Her use of culture and geographical place locates her connections to family and were reminiscent of narratives of diaspora. Amma zealously explores her past, creating new memories and further understanding why she came into care—something not all children are able to do. Mixed young people in care who experience transience are less likely to become successful care leavers as frequent movement diminishes their capacity for resilience and broken attachments dislocate them from consistent support. Transience is not solely a feature of mixed race children; high rates of disruption are a consequence of Children's Social Care departments making decisions driven by financial constraints.

Placing children with white carers is a natural circumstance for many mixed children who tend to come from white mother families. Interrogating some of the assumptions about white mothering can lead to more stable placements. Accepting the role of white mothering is the first step in acknowledging that mixed children have a different family experience to black children. White carers can have support in the community to share cultural practices with foster children so they grow up with knowledge of their specific heritage.

Placing children in foster homes outside of the local authority reduces contact with social workers and increases risk as children become isolated and have reduced contact due to distance. Ensuring they have the means to contact advocacy or are seen alone in order to talk honestly is vital. The over-application of resilience as a concept negates poor practice and its use needs moderation as children are at very real risk in the care system. Tragically, Amma's story is all too common; her removal from home and the hope of finding a new and better family have been disastrous. Her transience through care is full of neglect and further abuse; separation from her siblings and the source of support they offer each other and movement through almost twenty varying care placements results in her returning home to her mother and sleeping in a tent in the back garden. The role of care is to offer care. Perhaps its role has changed over the years towards more short-term placements; however, some children need either support and intervention to stay with their birth family or a new permanent family much earlier. It is clear that the care system is failing Amma and too many others like her.

References

Alibhai-Brown, Y. (2001). *Mixed feelings*. London: The Women's Press.

Barn, R. (1993). *Black children in the public care system*. London: Batsford.

Barn, R., Andrew, L., & Mantovani, N. (2005). *Life after care: A study of the experiences of young people from different ethnic groups*. York: University of York, Joseph Rowntree Foundation.

Barn, R., & Harman, V. (2006). A contested identity: An exploration of the competing social and political discourse concerning the identification and positioning of young people of inter-racial parentage. *British Journal of Social Work, 36*(8), 1309–1324.

Batmanghelidjh, C. (2006). *Shattered lives*. Gateshead: Athenaeum Press.

Biehal, N., Clayden, J., Stein, M., & Wade, J. (1992). *Resilience and young people leaving care. Prepared for living? A survey of young people leaving the care of three local authorities*. London: National Children's Bureau.

Biehal, N., & Wade, J. (1996). Looking back, looking forward: Care leavers, families and change. *Children and Youth Services Review, 18*(4–5), 425–445.

Caballero, C., Edwards, R., & Puthussery, S. (2008). *Parenting 'mixed' children: Negotiating difference and belonging in mixed race, ethnicity and faith families*. London: Joseph Rowntree Foundation.

Cohen, P. (1994). Yesterday's words, tomorrow's world: From the racialisation of adoption to the politics of difference. In I. Gaber & J. Aldridge (Eds.), *Culture, identity and transracial adoption: In the best interests of the child*. London: Free Association Books.

Gilroy, P. (1993a). *Small acts: Thoughts on the politics of Black cultures*. London: Serpent's Tail.

Gilroy, P. (1993b). *The Black Atlantic: Modernity and double consciousness*. London: Verso.

Kuhn, A. (1995). *Family secrets acts of memory and imagination*. London: Verso.

Levy, A. (1995). *Small island*. London: Picador.

Nunno, M., & Motz, J. (1988). The development of an effective response to the abuse of children in out-of-home care. *Child Abuse & Neglect, 12*(4), 521–528.

Ritchie, C. (2005). Looked after children: Time for change? *British Journal of Social Work, 35*(5), 761–767.

Selvon, S. (1956). *The lonely Londoners.* London: Alan Wingate.

Skeggs, B. (1997). *Formations of class and gender.* London: Sage.

Stein, M., & Carey, K. (1986). *Leaving care.* Oxford: Blackwell.

Stein, M. (2005). *Resilience and young people leaving care: Overcoming the odds.* York: Joseph Browntree Foundation, University of York.

Thoburn, J., Norford, L., & Rashid, S. P. (2000a). *Permanent family placement for children of minority ethnic origin.* London: Jessica Kingsley.

Thoburn, J., Wilding, J., & Watson, J. (2000b). *Family support in cases of emotional abuse and neglect.* London: The Stationery Office.

Unterhalter, E. (2000). Gendered diaspora identities: South African women, exile and migration. In S. Ali, K. Coate, & W. Goro (Eds.), *Global feminist politics: Identities in a changing world* (pp. 107–125). London: Routledge.

Waterhouse, R. (2000). *Lost in care* (Report of the tribunal of enquiry into the abuse of children in care in the former county council areas of Gwynedd and Clwyd since 1974). London: The Stationary Office.

Websites

Fayle, J. (2015, May). *Placement disruption.* www.nafp.cp.uk

The Children Act 1989. http://www.opsi.gov.uk/acts/acts1989/ukpga_19890041_en_4

The state of the nation report 1 children in care and care leavers survey. www.childrenscommissioner.gov.uk (accessed on 13 November 2015).

8

The Leaving Care Transition

Lucy   They told me I'm going to a mother and baby unit to look after my child. Telling me they could decide whether you can have your child or not, out of all these placements, that was the worst.

Fiona   How old was Ocean?

Lucy   Three days old. Just born. A lot of girls come there and left without their baby. Social services come, take their child. I was quite lucky to leave with Ocean. A lot of the girls fell asleep with their babies in the bed and social services come and take them.

Fiona   You did well.

Lucy   I said, 'You're mad. None of you lot is taking my child off me. I'll escape.'

Fiona   What made you different to the other girls?

Lucy   I was determined. I wouldn't let her go through what I went through. Man, that was madness. So, I said, 'You know what? Let me just do it and look after her', and that's what I done. Didn't pay any mind to all them girls just arguing. Them girls lost their children because they decided on using arguments, bitching with other girls, saying, 'I fucked your baby father,' and all this. One of them girls had sex with my daughter's dad.

© The Editor(s) (if applicable) and The Author(s) 2016

F. Peters, *Fostering Mixed Race Children*,

DOI 10.1057/978-1-137-54184-0_8

Lucy's pregnancy and early days of mothering make her subject to close surveillance by social workers not only due to her age (seventeen) but the nature of her relationship with Ocean's father. Statistics on female care leavers show that teenage pregnancy rates are three times the average and 22 % of teenage girls in care or leaving care are pregnant (2014). However, one in ten lose their own children to the care system. Sometimes, pregnancy can be a positive choice for care leavers with no qualifications; motherhood offers status and maturity, a sense of purpose and direction (Haydon 2003).

> Risk factors include high levels of family disruption, low parental supervision, poor school attendance and an associated lack of aspiration. (Burghart 2014)

Lucy experiences the power of social workers to remove her baby and awareness of having to capitulate to their rules and regulations in order to raise her daughter. Her awareness of following the rules comes from over fifteen years in residential and foster care homes, where she has learnt to bend to the regulations which manage her life. Lucy is resolute and her determination to keep her daughter out of care is admirable, as it is a challenge for care leavers to successfully parent their children. The British Association of Adoption and Fostering (BAAF) estimate that children and young people who have been in care are sixty-six times more likely to have their own children taken into care (2010). One of Lucy's aunts lived in foster care as a child. Lucy's cousins, aunts, and all five of her brothers have been in care at some point. The majority of the men in her family, including her dad, have been to prison. The inter-generational cycle of institutionalized care in families puts future generations of children at risk even before they are born.

The strength Lucy demonstrates at age seventeen, to keep her child despite the pressures to fit in with her peers, shows determination and independent thought and marks her out as able to accept her role as a parent and be responsible for her child—admirable qualities in someone so young who has no real concrete experience of a stable, secure family life. Lucy is leaving the support network of care, which has been a protective mechanism during her early years, but is now one which she experiences as restrictive—as she states, 'I can't wait to leave.' She has healthy feelings towards her corporate parents and has had adequate preparation for independence.

This chapter examines the very specific challenges that she and perhaps other mixed race young women may face as care leavers through an exploration of how appearance, gender, and heterosexuality intersect and shape care leaving experiences and early adult independence. Mixedness as a visible identification underpins social and cultural discourses surrounding perceptions of female desirability, sexuality, and beauty. Lucy's visibility and appearance as mixed race constitutes the limits and boundaries of her identification through specific types of encounters and behaviours in public spaces, which increase her vulnerability.

Pen Portrait

Lucy is now twenty years old and living in semi-independent accommodation with her baby, Ocean, age twenty months. The ground floor garden flat is heaving with toys and is clean and organized. She enjoys being a full-time mum, but has ambitions to work and is mature, responsible, and thoughtful, always trying to plan ahead and committed to giving her child a better start in life. She is in a busy phase of life, arranging the move into a new flat, and is reliant on help whenever possible.

Lucy's parents are both Jamaican. She describes herself as black but her referral from Children's Social Care states she is mixed race—her appearance somewhat belies her heritage: she is very fair-skinned with long, straight, black hair. Lucy came into care because of domestic violence and has been in many, many types of placements over her fifteen years in care. She has five brothers who were also in care. She lives near her large extended family and keeps in touch with her parents, on her terms.

In order to find and secure her new flat Lucy uses the online service to bid on council and housing association properties. She is fairly high up the housing list because of her care leaver status. It is a time-consuming and uncertain process as the best properties go quickly and she does not always have a reliable online connection. Eventually her bid on a new build flat, three miles away, is successful. Her uncle accompanies her to sign for the flat and collect the keys. Lucy juggles utility providers, arranges moving dates, packs, orders and meets furniture deliveries, puts together flat pack furniture, all the time caring for Ocean. Quelling her excitement over moving in are issues with money: applying for housing benefit, paying the rent, moving in grants for furniture, and so on. Reluctant to ask for help and unable to get the right advice, she put back the moving date several times.

Putting the Body in its Place

Lucy spoke about criminality and danger in relation to events which took place on nearby council housing estates. The status of her narratives as truth accounts is irrelevant. It is their pertinence as a topic that offers an opportunity to examine how Lucy understands her identifications through narrative production. Such narrative co-production is useful in highlighting not only the content of the story but also why the story is told. The analysis of the interview as both a resource and topic shows the value of the council estate as a symbolic representation in how Lucy understands and chooses to share her life. She presents the council estate as a place of fear, vulnerability, and danger.

Lucy   That girl has done a runner; she left London. He broke up with her and next thing you know, petrol poured through the door, only one exit on the fifth floor the kids couldn't get out or anything.

Fiona   How many children were in the house?

Lucy   So, we got back. Six kids. We saw so many police. We stayed there for three nights waiting. He thought he saw her a couple of months back in a club, but, as he went through the club, she disappeared. I had a big fight with her outside the studio. Them times, I was a little bitch. The girl must have went for my face. I threw her against the wall. Me and her went through the window together. The police got called and they hauled me off her. I calmed down, so the girl spat in my face. I had handcuffs on and I just flew at her and fly kicked her in her face. She was obsessed with him; he couldn't even go toilet by himself. The girl started stalking him. This girl knew we had been friends since seven years old. She thought we were doing a ting.

Lucy shares her relationship with a friend who lost his family in a fire and who is now godfather to Ocean. She met him when she used to sing and he was a rapper; they performed together. Lucy considers the space of the estate as partly responsible for the children becoming trapped. There was only one exit on the fifth floor. Lucy begins talking about two murders on a notorious local council estate. She knew one of the victims well, as they were close in age and grew up together. Again, the safety of the estate, through its physical space and its ability to trap its inhabitants into vulnerability and danger, is a strong theme.

Fiona   Do you think that what happened to her would not have hap-
         pened if cameras were there to see it, to stop it?
Lucy   Nah, because he grabbed her, but he done it devious by grabbing
         her and took her up the back way. It's stupid the police and the
         community can't see that them young black mums are at risk.
         They got ber bars on their doors to keep people out, man.
Fiona   I've never been there. What's it like?
Lucy   There are five levels and four staircases. Untold things can hap-
         pen. Basically three houses and one balcony. The lifts hardly
         work. You need cameras on them stairs to watch who is coming
         in that block.

The role of the estate in Lucy's narrative continues to centre on danger, this time through how gender invites a greater vulnerability to risk of crime. Lucy worries about other young, black women and mums on the estates who are vulnerable to crime and in need of protection. She is involved in a campaign to improve lighting, add CCTV cameras, and increase surveillance on the estate in order to deter criminal activity, or at least identify the perpetrators. The campaign forces the council to take responsibility for its neglect and abandonment of the residents.

Fiona   So, your friend who was attacked, if there was a camera, it would
         have been seen?
Lucy   Nah, don't think so. They put the gun in the bin, took the bala-
         clava off, and put it in the bin; the boy in court was no more
         than fifteen that shot him.

Fiona	Did someone older tell him to do it?
Lucy	Must've been. A fifteen-year-old boy isn't just going to do that. It was all over a dog, you know. His dog. That's how sick people are, killing black people for their things.
Fiona	They wanted to steal his dog?
Lucy	The guy wanted his puppy, a pit bull—a blue one. They're worth over £600. That's all they killed him for.

Lucy's friend was chased through the stairwells and, upon reaching the door of his flat, was murdered. The killers stole his dog. Among young men, many so-called dangerous dogs are kept as status symbols but these dogs serve another poverty-driven function: protection from violence. In this instance the dog was so highly prized as to be the causal factor in her young friend's murder. Lucy's three narratives open up a discursive space to examine how the lack of protection in areas she frequents constitutes boundaries of fear and danger.

Field Diary 12/04/2008 Lucy's narratives scare me, they are replete with violence, she knows hardened people and I am with her during a chat between her and her aunt which she talked about luring the local racist into her home to 'give her a good beating'. I am hesitant in our encounters.

These incidents all happened on neglected council housing estates, which are spaces of vulnerability and danger and a causal factor in how specific types of bodies and the values attached to them are acted upon. The lack of police protection and surveillance technologies and the architecture of the building all place the inhabitants at risk. The increasing vulnerability of the residents leads to crimes of a serious and brutal nature. Lucy's fourth story places her in the space of the council estate as she negotiates the presence of others and manages the visibility and vulnerability of her own body safely in what she understands as dangerous territory.

Lucy	When I left there, that's when I met Rick.
Fiona	How did you meet him?
Lucy	You know what? It wasn't even funny. I was in Hackney. Yeah, it was summer and I was in Hackney and all the girls had their

shorts on and their vest tops and we all had flip flops on, walking round the estate and he must have driven round in his car, music blasting out and everyone turned round and looked at him and, all of a sudden, he must have drove round the block and I thought, 'What's this man doing?' He come out the car, come right up to me and grabbed my hand and goes, 'Can I talk to you?' I say, 'Yeah, what's up?' He goes, 'Can I talk to you in private?' The next thing you know, he took my number and I took his. He said, 'Ring me when you want, yeah.' I said, 'All right.' I never rang him for about five months. I see him again. He said, 'How come you didn't ring?' I said, 'I lost your number.' He said, 'No you haven't.' I said, 'Yeah, I did. Sorry.' Next thing you know he turned round and says, 'You want to go out for something to eat?' We went out for lunch, went out for everything, yeah. Then, I found out I was pregnant. I didn't want to tell him, but he guessed. I was being sick in the morning and he goes, 'I'm taking you doctors.' We went to the hospital. They go do you want the good news or the bad? The woman goes, 'You're pregnant,' and we looked at each other and he goes, 'You happy?' and I slapped him and goes, 'You fucking bastard.'

Lucy is sixteen years old and living in a semi-independent hostel, close to the council estate, when she meets Rick. Her suspicion as she watches him drive around, get out of the car, and walk towards her is born from curiosity not romance. She questions his motives. He grabs her hand. She takes his number but does not call him. She is uninterested and it is only when they meet again five months later that they begin dating—he buys her a meal. The narrative density signals that 'lunch and everything' leads to a sexual relationship and pregnancy. Within the space of the estate a specific set of heterosexual and gendered practices emerge, underpinning this particular space as a site in which hierarchies of power produce social relations.

Place invokes social relations that are both a creation and production of those who inhabit and move through those spaces. Specific spaces inform and structure how people interact with one another across social hierarchies. The stratification of council housing, as a site of poverty and government neglect, has its own laws and regulations and can reveal oppressive practices through the negotiation of sexuality, race, age, gender, and status and the value attached to specific types of bodies.

Council housing estates are places controlled by men, and the current postcode wars reflect the emphasis on ownership and territory over poor urban areas. Young men are unable to encroach on another gang's territory without fear. This is not to suggest that women are absent from gang membership, simply that the association with men as primary subjects in and of such spaces has been the topic of more attention. Certain types of men are able to move through estates more easily than others. Rick is the man on the estate who is invisible because of the power he wields through his age and status, which (in an environment where black men die young) is valuable. He is in fact highly visible, but what he is able to do remains 'unseen' by others in a metaphorical sense. He is feared by women for his history of sexual assault, kidnap, and rape of a minor and revered and feared by men for his power, wealth, and evasion from prosecution. Rick is divested of race; as a black man on the estate, his power to move through the geography is unhampered by other men. Blackness, money, status, and age are powerful and fear-inducing on the estate. The relationship Rick enters into with Lucy is possible through the lack of official regulation and wider social discourses surrounding public space. His value and invisibility is tied to the council estate in which he is able to control other people. Rick's specific identity is under-valued in wider society and is thus of greater value in this marginal space of the estate in which he may act relatively free of intervention.

Doreen Massey (1994) claims that all social identities, social categories, and hierarchies articulate, in some way, with place and are routed through discourses such as race, gender, and class. The estate is a site of symbolic power negotiable through gender and race. The structuring of Lucy's position in relation to Rick's is through how the values of their bodies act upon their environment, and underpinning this are ideas surrounding visibility. Such freedom of movement in space is theorized by Puwar (2004) through attention to in/visibility of bodies. Invoking constitutive boundaries applies to raced bodies (in places not usually associated with hegemonic socio-cultural understandings of power through place) and shifts attention to the intersection of race, gender, and sexuality.

Processes of invisibility and visibility help us to understand the nuanced dynamics of subtle forms of exclusion as well as the basis for differentiated inclusion ... they have a social position in (occupational) space that is tenuous, a contradictory location marked by dynamics of in/visibility. (Puwar 2004: 58)

When a body is empty of its gender or race, it becomes invisible and its privilege as normative is to be seen without corporeality, and this is how white male bodies are conceptualized. Puwar (2004) claims that the relationship between space and bodies is characterized by a constellation of social practices and behaviours that permit and deny particular types of bodies. Social spaces are not blank and open for anybody to occupy. While all bodies can enter, certain types of bodies are natural occupants of specific positions. Some bodies have the right to belong but others trespass in accordance with how space and bodies are imagined—they are out of place not being the somatic norm; they are 'space invaders' (2004: 8). Women in public spaces that have been designated male spaces are abject and constitute space in ways that embody their gender and sexuality, making them highly visible.

Male spaces bound by class can be sites neglected by wider social mores or are sites marked by the dominance of men who can act without scrutiny. When women negotiate these spaces they can be routinely reminded of their embodiment through wolf whistling, sexual remarks, and chatting up or other practices that mark the body as gendered and exclude it on that basis. The presence of Lucy and her girlfriends walking through the estate in 'flip-flops, shorts, and vest tops' defines the boundaries of who can pass through the space and be invisible. The contentious issue of whether women wearing revealing clothes invite sexual advances is much debated in legal and social discourse. Clothes signify the performance of one version of adolescent, heterosexual femininity. Lucy's account of her presence on the estate highlights what has become the norm for the estate, which is the right of men to inhabit the space freely. The bodies of young women on the estate are not the somatic norm; they are of the space, but not constitutive of its limits; rather, they draw its boundaries. The young women act back upon the estate through appearance, gender, and sexuality and expose its male constitution through their performance coercing a response. Lucy's understanding of space is through how the council estate structures risk and vulnerability and is a place which conceals danger and death through lack of protection and surveillance.

> What constitutes an adolescent girl—the version that constructs who she is seen as and who she can be—links her in a variety of ways to her body, in terms of becoming the object of sexual positioning as the recipient of a visual definition of self. (Frost 2001: 81)

The stratification and social relations of the estate and the visible materiality of the young women's bodies define them as the sexual objects of male attention. This extends through attention to the visual grammar of race and takes account of who is the object of the gaze and who gazes. Lucy is the object of Rick's gaze as the most sexually appealing. Why she is the most appealing has its basis in the social construction of categories through visible difference (Lucy appears mixed and passes as mixed). The active nature of race-making sustains through attention to the performance of the gendered body, mixedness, age, and beauty ideals.

Making Mixedness Work

Theorizing the experiences of black women entails acknowledging that standards of femininity and beauty structure sexual desirability, and skin colour, hair texture, and facial features are intrinsic to that. While analyses of the black subject reject the biological essentialism of identity (Gilroy 1993a, b) and argue for blackness as a socio-political and cultural construction, essentialism continues to inform everyday practices of race-making. In everyday experiences, skin, hair, and features matter; they constitute belonging and underpin gender, (hetero)sexuality, age, and geographical location (space). These identifications inform and are informed by socio-cultural representations and constructions of status and power that underpin media and culture.

> *Field Diary 5/5/2008 The intersection of mixedness and femaleness is exploited by men and women alike and my position as a mixed race woman observing and documenting Lucy's life brings attention to how her life is exploited in this process and how ugly it feels to document that.*

Lucy's mixed appearance and her being chosen by Rick as the *one* is no coincidence. What is acceptable as beautiful and (hetero)sexually attractive among black women remains within an 'essentialist construction of black womanhood' signified by hair length and texture, skin shade, and parentage (Weekes 1997: 114). Definitions of beauty make whiteness the norm and self-effacing practices among dark-skinned black and Asian women, such as skin bleaching and hair straightening, offer evidence that heterosexual desirability has its roots in white European beauty ideals. Beauty is light skin and straight hair; evidence of this is the six billion dollar industry supplying African-American women with wigs and weaves made from the hair of Brazilian and Indian women.

Lucy's cultural heritage is Jamaican and both of her parents are black, yet her skin, hair, and features suggest mixedness and she passes as mixed due to misrecognition, a common aspect of her everyday experience. Jamaicans acknowledge their mixed heritage and during independence in 1962 the leaders chose the motto 'Out of Many One People'. This motto reflects the history of an island that has been mixing race for centuries and acknowledges that nation rather than colour is paramount in understanding identity. Not that mixedness can be solely understood or recognized through visible appearance as racial difference, but that the constitutive elements of mixedness are ambiguous. These elements are not routed solely through appearance or through cultural practices but are intrinsic to how beauty is measured, and Rick's selection of Lucy is due to her more culturally desirable appearance—and her age.

Race is a sign of visible difference read off the body that serves as its text. The visible racial differences of skin and hair are signifiers or indicators of unseen qualities such as morality or sexuality and can be said to constitute an inner schema embedding DNA. Race is one of many constructs that signify difference or sameness and is relational to other variables such as gender, sexuality, location, and class; such signifiers are known as sliding (Cohen 1994). Race is made among people to assign others with identities that characterize them through a bodily schema and further define and inform the social construction of categories. In everyday experience, Lucy's appearance signals an identification through skin, which mobilizes gender and sexuality in specific contexts and makes meanings accessible through discursive constructions of race-making and the discourse surrounding the sexuality and sexualization of mixed women.

Gendering Mixedness: Ghosts of the Past in the Present

How mixed race women become tied to their bodies emerges during American and Caribbean plantation slavery and has an enduring legacy seen in popular culture. The sexual exploitation of black and mixed women was justifiable through hierarchies of racial classification. Racial mixing was a necessary economic tool of slavery for reproducing the population. Slavery endured for four centuries and the increasing population of mulattos, quadroons, and octoroons swelled the ranks and ensured a continuing labour supply.[1] However, the increasing numbers of mulatto slaves who have white fathers posed a dilemma for the continuation of slavery as claims to the economic wealth of plantation owners threaten the maintenance of prosperity and power. Legislation was passed and the 'One-Drop Law'[2] asserted that, despite white skin, a social classification of black would apply to anyone with one drop of black blood, thus ensuring the labour supply. The growing mixed race population became a buffer between blacks and whites and afforded greater privileges—house slaves as opposed to field slaves, for example—but this made mulatto women more vulnerable to rape within plantation homes (Reuter 1918). The intersection of sexuality and race mixing led to the female mulatto body becoming symbolic of sexual exploitation and proof that the colour line had been crossed.

The ghosts of slavery, ideas, representations, articulations, and actions that underpin social relations have left their remnants in contemporary culture. For example, during slavery, mulatto women held social events for white men to meet other mulatto women, known as 'Quadroon Balls'. The aim of the events was for the women to secure financial support from white men in exchange for long-term sexual services—a practice known as Placage.[3] This racial dynamic continues to influence contemporary and popular culture. For example, Halle Berry, Oscar winner for her role in

---

[1] Mulatto is one black parent and one white parent, quadroon is one mulatto parent and one black parent, and octoroon is one mulatto parent and one white parent.

[2] One drop of black blood led to a black classification.

[3] Placage was a recognized extralegal system by which European men entered into the equivalent of common law marriages with women of colour.

the film *Monster's Ball*, plays a woman who exchanges being taken care of financially in return for a sexual relationship. Berry's Oscar win for her role confirms that her mixedness is well suited to the demands of mainstream American audiences in which the sexual exploitation of mixed women feeds into the marketplace as a commodity. The social relations that emerge through the female mixed body are discernible through historic remnants, and these traces have consequences for race-making in contemporary popular and cultural life.

The prevalence of and preference for mixed race women to appear as sexually provocative dancers in hip hop videos, known as 'video hoes', has been documented by Sharpley-Whiting (2008). An article written by Searle (2010) refers to an interview Kanye West did with *Essence* magazine in which West made the following comments: 'If it wasn't for race mixing there'd be no video girls … Me and most of our friends like mutts a lot. Yeah, in the hood they call 'em mutts' (West 2006). (West's daughter with Kim Kardashian was born in 2013 and she is mixed.) The 'mixed race girl syndrome',[4] whereby desire is fed by discursive constructions of what light skin means—desirability, beauty, status, and sexual voracity—informs British popular culture. These discourses underpin how young women construct and adapt their identifications in the presence of men, working within configurations of race, sex, and appearance and the use of their bodies as a commodity for economic gain. The intersection of sex and gender applies to women of all races and appearances, but, for mixed race women, there are racially specific factors which underpin notions of beauty and desirability and increase earlier sexualization.

The National Crime Victimization Survey figures (NAWS 1998) from the Bureau of Justice statistics confirm that 'Multiracial women are significantly more likely to be victims of rape and attempted rape at a rate double that of Caucasians and five times that of Asian women' (cited in Jackson Nakazawa 2003: 136). Their prevalence in advertising and popular culture due to the equal opportunity of objectification means they are victims of their sexual desirability.

An overpowering image of Rick cruising the council estate, projecting a specific version of masculinity, feeds into these models of socio-cultural

---

[4] *Little Baby Jesus*, performed in 2010.

practices and relations that happen in urban Britain. The estate is situated near the semi-independent residential home and, as the girls from the home meander through the estate, they become vulnerable to predatory tendencies of men. It is known that children's residential care facilities are targets for pimps who can lure girls into prostitution (Nash and Cusick 2004).[5] The lack of adult supervision, poor regulation of public spaces, and the position of homes near council estates increases vulnerability. Lucy's vulnerability increases at the intersection of her status as a 'young female care leaver with a mixed race appearance' living near a large council estate.

Performing Through Misrecognition

The sexualization of mixed race women is different to that of both black and white women and mediated through popular cultural forms and ideas underpinning racial classification. While out with Lucy, collecting boxes at the nearby Tesco supermarket to prepare for her house move, we meet her maternal aunt. Lucy's appearance in her family is due to her paternal grandmother who is also very light skinned with long dark hair and, while growing up, she was said to resemble her. As the only child in the family with such light skin and straight hair she is visibly different to her family. Lucy's aunt begins a conversation about Lucy's appearance in relation to her skin tone and hair texture—she feels that if she were to change her own appearance, she would have longer, straighter, easier to manage 'good' hair and pointed out that Lucy's hair is perfect.

Aunt If I could have your hair I would.
Lucy Yeah, I know you would.
Aunt Your skin is too white, though. I wouldn't want to be so white.
Lucy Thanks for that.
Aunt You na look black.

---

[5] Nash and Cusick's (2004) report 'Sex Industry and Sexual Exploitation' found that residential care homes were targets for the formation of a network of young girls being abused through prostitution by a man known as Martin Malone. His accomplices included an employee from Children's Social Services.

The denigration of Lucy's skin tone and the elevation of her hair texture is symbolic of mixedness as a contestable and ambiguous social position and classification. 'Good Hair'[6] is straight, long, and easy to manage, containing no traces of Afro curl or texture; it is smooth and shiny. Good hair, thought to be more desirable and one aspect of being more acceptable in mainstream culture in a Western society, elevates status and social position. Many black women relax their hair and remove the curl, weave it to cover up the curl, and believe that the chances for jobs, partners, and success are greater without Afro hair. The distribution and retail of products in the hair industry for black women in Britain is mostly under control of Asian companies who import and sell to a demanding African and Caribbean female population. Lucy's aunt has Afro hair with tell-tale signs of relaxing or weaves, which damage the hairline, leading to hair loss and permanent baldness. The symbolic and political position of hair in mainstream understandings and practices among the majority of African-Caribbean women underpins Lucy's hair as desirable; it is naturally straight, thick, and long with no sign of Afro curl. Hence, her Aunt thinks it perfect—it resembles a good quality weave which can cost thousands of pounds.

However, Lucy's skin is the subject of derision and while skin-lightening creams are popular they are never used to eliminate all traces of melanin—just to lighten skin so it has a tan or glow. Lucy is very pale and her aunt ensures she knows that 'too white skin' is undesirable. Skin is one way to measure beauty, and the growing attention and valorization of mixed race people is part of a narrative that suggests 'tan skinned' (neither too white nor dark) is most desirable, and we certainly see this in relation to white women who use sun-beds, fake tans, and bronzing products. Mixed race is becoming the standard by which beauty is measured, and increasing attention to the unique look of mixed people and emphasis on 'good hair' and skin feed into a gendered discourse concerning beauty.

For Lucy the cultural enactment and performance of her culture, sexuality, and gender is part of her ambiguity and misidentification, leading

---

[6] See Chris Rock's film of the same name.

to a performance of self which she uses to secure a recognizable and socially legitimate identification. As Scales-Trent claims,

> My very existence demonstrates there is a slippage between the seemingly discreet categories black and white. It is at this point of slippage that we can clearly see that race is not a biological fact but a social construct ... creating and maintaining, a racial identity takes a lot of effort on my part, and on the part of others. Race is not an act of imagination. It is a very demanding verb. (1995: 3)

Lucy's mixed appearance gives rise to her misrecognition. Her cultural belonging is rooted in her Jamaican family and their heritage and practices. It is hard to say conclusively whether her way of maintaining race, by invoking specific practices that confer social legitimacy, is born out of her many instances of misrecognition or if it is notable because of her appearance. Misrecognition and subsequent lack of social legitimacy coerces a cultural performance, since mixedness neither adequately nor accurately captures Lucy's heritage or identification. What work does Lucy do to claim her Jamaican heritage, to embody it in ways that activate and mobilize race—as Scales-Trent (2005) claims, to 'create and maintain' race? Lucy expresses and performs her familial Jamaican heritage, through cultural practices, into a recognizable identity. Lucy's mixed appearance, age, gender, and sexuality create both recognition and social legitimacy and enable her to make specific choices of heterosexual dating partners.

Match-Making and Dating

Lucy and her current British-Jamaican boyfriend, Ron, are standing outside his workplace on a balmy evening just two streets away from where she lives. Lucy uses Patois (an English-based Creole language with West African influences) while talking with him. Rick, Ocean's father, has been sitting in his car and watching Lucy's flat at six in the morning, possibly checking for the presence of another man. Lucy is delivering a commentary on Rick's past criminal activity and spells in prison. Ron seems like a nice guy and has worked in the local hardware shop for ten years. Lucy's performance, in the context of her sexual relationship, anchors her social legitimacy through a cultural performance that mobilizes and maintains race, underpinning it with her Jamaican nationality. Lucy's use of language, reliance on gender and sexuality in the context of present and past heterosexual relationships, and invocation of the worst aspects of black masculinity position her as Jamaican. Lucy relies on a cultural performance to create a racialized self, one which is not anchored through her appearance.

Butler's work on performance and gender claims that masculinity and femininity are 'scripts, which are animated by the work of the body' (1993: 111). Butler's premise is that there is no essence to gender; it is not a fact, but is always in the process of becoming. Our gender identities are an accomplishment, an act that we constitute through performance and are 'renewed, revised, and consolidated through time' (ibid.: 111). The acts are not natural, but, over time, they become so through repetition, making them appear natural and giving the illusion of an abiding, gendered self, amounting to a set of cultural fictions of what is a real man or real woman. 'The gendered body acts its part in a culturally restricted corporeal space and enacts interpretations within the confines of already existing directives' (Puwar 2004: 80). Lucy's repertoire of cultural fictions for how she secures both misrecognition and ambiguity through culture and gender are a useful strategy for survival as a heterosexual woman living at the boundaries of what it means to be both black and mixed. Within a cultural geography in which dominant black cultural forms both elevate and denigrate her body through her gender and her appearance, she is able to access an additional ethnic and cultural resource of Jamaican culture, which secures social legitimacy through a recognizable repetition. Lucy creates an ethnically and racialized self (one somewhat denied through her mixed appearance) which grants social legitimacy. She uses cultural practices to perform a specific type of heterosexual self.

Lucy   They're going to Janie's.
Fiona   Is her partner African?
Lucy   Yeah, not something I would go for.
Fiona   Not your type?
Lucy   Hell no.

Fiona   They're very handsome.
Lucy   Nah man, I don't go for African.
Fiona   Where is Jerome from?
Lucy   Jamaica. His mum's from Jamaica, his dad from Barbados, he ain't no Yardie and he ain't no African. I like him the way he is. I wouldn't change him.

One afternoon several weeks later as I drop Lucy off at her new flat we see her neighbour, Janie, and her African partner walking towards us. Lucy's refusal to date African men and the long-standing hostility from Caribbean people towards Africans and vice versa makes them an unlikely choice as a way to secure social legitimacy or social capital. (The hyphenation of African-Caribbean often fails to acknowledge this disjuncture or plays with the split and re-connection of what can be an ambivalent relationship.) Jerome is Lucy's new partner; they met locally and have been together for several weeks, although she has known him for a few months. Lucy's choice of sexual partners is older, Caribbean-British men and her sexual relationships are important as they offer her resources that are absent within both her peer network and her family relationships.

Leaving Care: Friends, Family, and Mothering

Lucy   She (mum) doesn't know my address. I said to her, 'I live somewhere nearby.' I haven't been over there yet.
Fiona   You're the only girl for your mum. Does she feel bad she doesn't have a proper relationship with you?
Lucy   She keeps telling me she wants a relationship with me. I just sit there and laugh at her. I don't need a relationship with her. I got my daughter. I don't worry about them, man. They got their little lives. I just leave them to it.

It is known that young people actively create social capital across social and family networks and across their ethnic and cultural identities (Reynolds 2009) to use for their own ends (Helve 2007). However, research findings with young people in gangs by Briggs (2009) suggest that young people can make social capital within social and peer group networks as they exhibit autonomy over their lives, solve conflicts, and cope with uncertainty en route to adulthood. Lucy's specific biography and the relationships she has with family and peers suggest that strategies and opportunities to build social capital are markedly reduced. The networks of family and friends she does have underpin her strategies for building a sense of community and stability. Hence, it is important that her family (despite their failures) like her choice of partner and are not antagonistic towards him. The wrong choice could make her position within the family network she continues to value even more tenuous. She regards the family networks as marking the boundaries within which she is able to act. However, she does not use these networks as sources of trust or reciprocity. Lucy holds the values of her family through ethnicity, cultural practices, family history, and biography as ways to build social capital. However, because her family networks are insecure and unstable she primarily relies on sexual relationships to build and maintain social and cultural capital, using her family's boundaries of acceptability to inform her of how to perform and live within a recognizable identification.

Social capital is a term that, although contentious, can be theorized in a number of ways to describe '[t]he values that people hold and the resources that they can access, which both result in and are the result of collective and socially negotiated ties and relationships' (Edwards et al. 2003: 2). While it might be expected that young people would first form these ties with family, young people in care and care leavers are often both physically and psychically separated from these links or trust has been broken and relationships are precarious and unstable. As co-operation, reciprocity, and trust are key moral categories of social capital, it is less likely that care leavers find such qualities among family members.

Field Diary July 2008: Through Lucy's moving-in process, I thought a lot about her official support network and wondered how I had become a key part of it. I wonder who would do this stuff if I wasn't around—it is slightly overwhelming and demanding. I often forget why I am really here and am too involved.

After Lucy moves into her flat she begins to see her family sporadically as she feels an obligation for Ocean to know her grandparents. Research shows care leavers may often try to establish contact with their birth family as they look for 'answers to their personal histories' (Stein et al. 2005: 122). The importance of family links and history highlights the importance young people place on accessing and building social capital (Bullock et al. 1993). Motherhood was renewing Lucy's relationships with her family but on her own terms and through a focus on adulthood and independence, not her own vulnerability to their poor choices and parenting. For Lucy to build social capital she has to be in a position where she is able to trust others within mutually beneficial relationships; the challenge is that Lucy has had a series of broken attachments to her family and will not trust them.

Fiona   You get on well with your dad, don't you?

Lucy   Yeah, since **** died, yeah. I got close to my family. Before they died, I used to hate him. I never used to get on with that man.

Fiona   How come?

Lucy   Basically, he left my mum when we were kids, so I never grew with him for a certain period of time. Then he came back, out the blue, wanting to be dad again. I didn't really know him, full well. I was like, 'Yeah, hi and bye.'

Her relationship with her dad is somewhat different—despite his being in prison for most of her childhood, she is able to connect with him. Her dad's form of parenting restricts the capital she is able to build through family networks as he places his needs before her ambitions or plans. For example, Lucy is thinking of getting a job and she holds up a yet to be completed application form for work as a Community Support Officer (CSO). She has made an effort to fill in some details. Her dad's response to her application to be a CSO was 'Don't grass me up or come to my yard looking for stuff.' Her father gets along with Lucy's partner, Jerome, a man of a similar age to himself. Lucy exhibits a desire to remain within the family, but this restricts what she is able to do within her own terms without incurring their disapproval.

Finding Value in Mothering

Lucy   At the moment, I do want my son, but not until she is bigger and can walk around a lot more because there is no way I will be pregnant and carrying her. And a double buggy? Not happening. If ever I got pregnant, I would use the sling.

Fiona   Or longer. Give yourself a chance to get some work, earn some money?

Lucy   Yeah, when Ocean's four, she will be at school and I can work full time and have more money.

Fiona   Are you looking forward to doing that?

Lucy   Yeah, but I want my son, but I know I would get another girl. I wouldn't get a boy. I would like someone for Ocean to grow up with and play with.

Fiona   What other ambitions have you got? What other things do you want to do?

Lucy   I want to work. I need to work. I'm going insane just looking after this girl, man. I need a life.

Fiona   You have had two years with her full time.

Lucy   My life is good. It's quiet. I got my daughter, no arguments, and no men jarring me; that's what I want. I want to see where it goes with me and Jerome. We been there for quite a while now. See what happens.

Motherhood and the importance she places on being a mother to her daughter enables Lucy to find meaning and focus on improving both their lives. She is content with the family she is re-making as it offers the opportunity for purpose and independence. Although she is going 'insane' being a mother, the options for employment are limited because she feels her lack of formal education is a barrier to her getting a job. Lucy is against going to college and being in a large group of learners in order to improve her skills.[7] Her poor level of literacy is due to transience and interruptions to her schooling. She believes it is embarrassing to return to education now or take literacy classes.

---

[7] The numerous changes of schools meant she finally refused to return to mainstream education at the age of fourteen and was sporadically educated in a Pupil Referral Unit.

Field Diary 21/11/2008: I worry that she will end up having another child because her work options are limited. She can't put off the inevitable independence that comes from work but her fears about her literacy not being good enough hold her back. Her dad's disapproval doesn't help—she is maintaining those bonds at too high a cost. Financially, while on benefits, she has free childcare. If she was working, she'd pay.

Lucy's two-bedroom flat is in a new build on the outskirts of her previous semi-independent flat and is home to a few other young mums. These relationships could be potential sources with which to build capital across peer networks. However, despite the potential of these friendships to offer support, they become a source of frustration as Lucy's parenting is at odds with the parenting of the other mums and this creates tension in their relationships. Lucy prides herself on her parenting skills. She gives to Ocean through depriving herself not only of material things but also freedom. Lucy rarely leaves Ocean with a babysitter and she and Jerome have never been on a date. The stories she relates about her peers demonstrate her frustration at their lack of parenting skills, interest, and care for their children. One young mum in the block likes to go out clubbing weekly and leaves her child regularly at Lucy's overnight. Janie, who lives downstairs, has a one-year-old son with cerebral palsy. Lucy is angry that Janie does not take him out to stimulate him, or to the baby clinic for his checks. Several weeks later, Lucy told me that Janie was pregnant again, but had been drinking neat vodka to get rid of the baby. The networks to build social capital are difficult for Lucy to negotiate as issues of trust and the differences in values and acceptable standards of parenting all complicate capital building. Lucy's peer networks are the other mothers in the block where she lives, and the varying standards of parenting are barriers to the creation of positive relationships. These peer networks do not enable trust or reciprocity but rather she feels used and frustrated. Lucy is building social capital and doing so in remarkable ways that utilize the skills she has learned through her care experiences: adaptability, control over her life within a limited framework, and, ironically, knowing how not to parent.

Lucy   I want to move from here, you know, because the girl downstairs, you know, she's doing my head in.

Fiona   Who? Janie?

Lucy   Yeah, me an' her got into a mad ruck the other day, you know.

Fiona   You two have got a love/hate relationship.

Lucy   You know what? She hit Ocean. I put her through her kitchen door. She hit her again, lost her temper with her. She made her fly across the room.

Fiona   What's she doing to her son down there?

Lucy   I don't even want to know. She hit her and you know what happened? I ended up giving her a black eye punching her in the mouth.

Fiona   Where were you when this happened?

Lucy   I was in the toilet. She shouted at her and all I see was Ocean flying across the room and she had a red mark across her face.

Field Diary 29/11/2008 Teenage mothers are a hard to reach group. They are both under enormous pressure: parenting, budgeting, and without any real support at a very young age—they are both like pressure cookers. It's no wonder they lose their children and repeat the cycle of care—no one should have to parent in such isolation. I think they don't reach out because they are fearful of their children being taken away or being judged.

Lucy   Yeah, every morning, when I wake up, and I feed Ocean and then, I take it. I feel sick in the morning. Last night, I was sick as hell, this morning.

Fiona   Maybe it was food.

Lucy   Nah, I didn't eat much last night.

Fiona   What have you said to Jerome?

Lucy   I didn't see him last night.

Fiona   So, he doesn't suspect anything

Lucy   Nah, but he's beginning to because in the morning I've been grouchy. He says, 'You all right?' I said, 'Yeah, I'm cool.'

Fiona   Lucy, what will you do if you are?

Lucy   Don't know. Probably keep it, knowing me. I want my son, don't I?

Fiona   Are you ready? You're a good mum. How would you manage two babies?

Lucy   Ocean is getting older so she's starting to do things by herself

Fiona   She's two…

Lucy is not pregnant on this occasion but she does get pregnant within the next two months. During the early stages of her pregnancy her relationship with Jerome goes through a bad patch. She is moody and does not want him around. She asks him to leave the flat, reassuring him that, once she is over the morning sickness, he can return. He never does return, although he supports her by going to the hospital for antenatal appointments. He is there at the birth of their son and spends the first few weeks with them as a family. Several months later, Lucy tells me that Jerome has a serious kidney complaint. He has been in hospital for several weeks.

In conclusion, a narrative co-production enables themes to emerge that offer new areas of enquiry into how participants make meaning and structure their worlds. The repetition of stories in relation to the council estate allows the symbolic role of space to structure ideas of vulnerability and danger in Lucy's narrative. Mixed race young women leaving care are made vulnerable to both early sexual maturity and sexual vulnerability due to the unregulated nature of public spaces and the increased freedom from supervision and protection as they move into semi-independent accommodation. Underpinning the social construction of mixed race women are historical cultural practices that inform current understandings of women in popular culture in relation to notions of beauty and desirability, which are tied to the body. Mixed race female care leavers need greater support in becoming aware of their sexual vulnerability due to the social construction of mixedness in both historical and contemporary popular culture.

Lucy demonstrates that engaging a cultural performance achieves social legitimacy within her sexual relationships and offers greater social legitimacy, which subverts her misrecognition as mixed. It allows her to build social capital and feel a sense of stability through relationships which, although transient, offer opportunities for motherhood in which social capital is secured. Lucy uses unique strategies to create social capital, using her sexuality, appearance, and fecundity in remarkable ways. Mothering offers Lucy the purpose and independence she needs to create an adult life on her own terms.

References

Briggs, D. (2009). 'True stories from bare times on road': Developing empowerment identity and social capital among urban minority ethnic youth in London. *Ethnic and Racial Studies, 33*(5), 851–887.

Bullock, R., Little, M., & Millham, S. (1993). *Going home: The return of children separated from their families*. Aldershot: Dartmouth.

Burghart. (2014). *Finding their feet; equipping care leavers to reach their potential*. London: Centre for Social Justice. http://www.centreforsocialjustice.org.uk/UserStorage/pdf/Pdf%20reports/Finding.pdf.

Butler, J. (1993). *Bodies that matter: On the discursive limits of 'sex'*. London: Routledge.

Cohen, P. (1994). Yesterday's words, tomorrow's world: From the racialisation of adoption to the politics of difference. In I. Gaber & J. Aldridge (Eds.), *Culture, identity and transracial adoption: In the best interests of the child*. London: Free Association Books.

Edwards, R., Franklin, J., & Holland, J. (2003). *Families and social capital: Exploring the issues* (Families and Social Capital ESRC Research Group Working Paper Series No. 1). London: South Bank University.

Frost, L. (2001). *Young women and the body a feminist sociology*. Hampshire: Palgrave.

Gilroy, P. (1993a). *Small acts: Thoughts on the politics of Black cultures*. London: Serpent's Tail.

Gilroy, P. (1993b). *The Black Atlantic: Modernity and double consciousness*. London: Verso.

Haydon, D. (2003). *Teenage pregnancy and looked after children/care leavers. Resource for teenage pregnancy co-ordinators*. London: Barnardo's.

Helve, H. (2007). Social capital and minority identities. In H. Helve & J. Bynner (Eds.), *Youth and social capital* (pp. 103–106). London: Tufnell Press.

Jackson Nakazawa, D. (2003). *Does anybody else look like me? A parent's guide to raising multiracial children*. Cambridge, MA: Perseus Books.

Massey, D. (1994). *Space, place and gender*. Minneapolis, MN: University of Minneapolis Press.

Nash, R., & Cusick, L. (2004). *Sex industry and sexual exploitation in Lewisham: Rapid assessment and response*. London: Centre for Research on Drugs and Health Behaviour, Imperial College.

Puwar, N. (2004). *Space invaders race: Gender and bodies out of place*. Oxford: Berg.

Reuter, E. B. (1918). *The mulatto in the United States*. Boston: Richard G. Badger.

Reynolds, T. (2009). Editorial introduction: Social capital and ethnic identity. *Ethnic and Racial Studies, 33*(5), 749–760.

Scales-Trent, J. (1995). *Notes of a White Black woman race, color, community*. University Park, PA: Pennsylvania State University Press.

Sharpley-Whiting, T. (2008). *Pimps up, ho's down: Hip Hop's hold on young Black women*. New York: New York University Press.

Stein, M. (2005). *Resilience and young people leaving care: Overcoming the odds*. York: Joseph Roundtree Foundation, University of York.

Weekes, D. (1997). Shades of blackness: Young Black female constructions of beauty. In H. S. Mirza (Ed.), *Black British feminism*. London: Routledge.

West, K. (2006, November 18). *Essence Magazine*. New York: Essence Communications.

Website

Searle, K. (2010). *'A yellow-ass nigga': Hip Hop and the 'mixed-race' experience*. http://www.mixedracestudies.org/wordpress/?tag=kevin-searle (accessed on 15 April 2010).

9

Learning from Mixed Race Children in Foster Care

One of Britain's most esteemed poets, Lemn Sissay, challenges us 'To shine a torch into those dark nooks and crannies, that institutions and organizations would rather we leave alone' (Sissay, 24/10/15). This book examines mixed race children's foster care experiences, through their personal narratives, to better understand the structural inequalities and crisis of Children's Social Care. As Mills suggests, 'A trouble is a private matter: values cherished by an individual are felt by him to be threatened. An issue often involves a crisis in institutional arrangements' (2000: 9). Two questions underpin the narrative focus. Firstly, how do young people make meaning from the discursive repertoires of the mixed classification in their foster care experiences? Secondly, in what ways are children's foster care experiences structured through understandings of mixedness? This book offers rich sociological insight into the experiences of mixed race children in care and into some of the Children's Social Care processes that underpin their experiences.

The crisis of the care system has a real impact on the lives and well-being of all children who are personally troubled by its systemic inadequacies. Children and young people in foster care recognize their own oppression and isolation and the failure of residential foster care to *care*

© The Editor(s) (if applicable) and The Author(s) 2016
F. Peters, *Fostering Mixed Race Children*,
DOI 10.1057/978-1-137-54184-0_9

for them. They expressed frustration at poor quality foster care, frequent changes of social workers, regulations around family contact, transience through poor placement matching, or financially driven placement disruption. The coercion to accept their circumstances came from limits on their consultation, and more needs to be done to ensure all children looked after by the local authority have a consistent, healthy, and trusting relationship that offers an opportunity to voice their opinions.

Research that considers children's views in the here and now, outside of the themes of fostering (despite them living in foster care), allows for deeper holistic understanding of the impact that processes and practices of foster care have on their everyday lives.

Tacking Assumptions About Mixed Families

The persistent and increasing over-representation of mixed race children living their childhoods in the residential and foster care systems informs us that the mixed classification is a specific disadvantage. What is urgently needed is a thorough examination of how and in what specific circumstances the process-led framework of Children's Social Care contributes to the high admissions and subsequent over-representation of mixed children in care. The continuing lack of social legitimacy afforded to mixed families underpins some decision-making practices in Children's Social Care. In particular, the legitimate and important role of white mothering of mixed children is seen as inadequate in addressing their children's cultural and ethnic needs. White, lone mothers living in impoverished conditions are more likely to have their mixed children placed in (foster) care. This systemic violence against mixed race families is part of an enduring cycle with roots in global politics, which aims to separate mixed race children from their families. Further research is desperately needed to root out assumptions about mixed families at their first contact with Children's Social Care in order to examine why such high care admission of mixed race children continues.

Attitudes and assumptions that mixed families are difficult to understand, not socially legitimate, or lack cultural knowledge guide interactions between parents and social workers. These parent and social worker dynamics are beset with power and status positions in which professional (and often middle-class) judgements undermine parents. The House of Commons report for looked-after children (MacLeod et al. 2008–2009) suggests one successful (American) method of an independent panel for assessing interactions between social workers and clients (parents). The panel is able to spot when class or race underpins decision-making and determine if discriminatory practices arise. These strategies to root out discrimination can improve practice, offer greater parity between social worker and family, and explore how assumptions (about race mixing and mixed families) can lead to negative intervention rather than whole family support. Further, it is vitally important that practitioners acknowledge and disrupt their own political positions and allegiances to ethnic and racial identifications as well as any judgements or assumptions, known or unknown, that impact their intervention with mixed families.

In *all* instances the mothers of the children in this book were living with domestic violence. Being a child witness of domestic violence can now be the sole reason for child removal. Further research is needed to explore the dynamics of mixed relationships and how race and gender underpin and shape how both men and women experience and cope with the pressures of such a relationship in their private and public lives.

There is a notable and disturbing absence of men and fathers when speaking of mixed race families who have children in foster care. The fathers of the children in this book, if at all present, were on the periphery of contact: lost touch completely, did not know the children were in care, or were in prison. Further research and persistent engagement with fathers in mixed families at the point of contact with Children's Social Care can deepen understanding and offer appropriate levels of support and intervention, possibly mitigating care admission. More needs to be done to include and encourage fathers to be a significant part of their children's lives.

Children in care often lose the asset upon which most young people continue to rely on beyond childhood and adolescence: their parents. Three participants express a desire to return home to their mothers, as they have understood their lives at home to be warm and loving even as they have described neglect and abuse. They offer redemption and empathy through acknowledging the living circumstances and pressures upon their parents. Amma, who probably had the most tragic start to life, had 'one wish, and that would be to live with my mum'. Children and young people in care no longer have their fiercest protectors at their side to advocate for them—as their parents are sidelined and occupy a marginal status due to their perceived inability to parent.

Fostering and Matching Mixed Race Children

The same race matching guidelines surrounding appropriate foster placements do not address the specific needs of mixed race children. The local authority guidelines in many boroughs maintain a focus on the child not 'standing out as visibly different' to the prospective foster family, conveying the assumption that families ought to look the same and that homogeneity is the standard by which family is legitimatized. Thus, the heterogeneity and visible differences within mixed families are deemed unacceptable. Mixed children in birth families do look visibly different from their parents and siblings and this is perfectly legitimate and ordinary. Relegating the emphasis of a child not being visibly different from carers removes barriers in long-term care planning and can offer greater stability and security for children needing permanence. Support for a child's ethnic, racial, and cultural heritage may be offered within the community. Further, acknowledging mixed children have a white parent, often the mother and primary caregiver, offers continuation of the primary socialization children are familiar with and removes the need for transience based upon the premise of a more ethnically and culturally appropriate match. White mothers can and have successfully parented mixed children for generations; but what is permissible in nature is denied in Children's Social Care.

Shared ethnic or racial backgrounds do not convey the cultural practices learned through family socialization, and most importantly they do not guarantee good foster care. The more *appropriate* ethnically matched placements in which mixed children are understood to learn their heritage, culture, and how to deal with racism are often unavailable due to a shortage of African and Caribbean foster carers. And if these carers are available it is highly likely that those placements would be prioritized for children with two same race parents. Many placements that meet the ethnic or cultural needs of children can in fact be at odds with how the children understand their identifications and cultural expressions, as was the case with Stealth and his ambivalent position towards his Jamaican heritage. Children in foster care often become cultural chameleons in their placements, because they are expected to embrace new habits and customs due to differences in the ethnic heritage and culture between child and carers, which takes time and patience to negotiate.

The matching process for fostering mixed children is more complex and needs more time; it takes empathy and a deep exploration of family relationships and history on both the maternal and paternal side, with practitioners learning about both the ethnic heritage and cultural practices of parents and grandparents. Closer attention to the individual holistic needs of the child will always result in placing the child in the most attentive, loving home and offering much needed stability. Factors such as cultural practices and ethnic heritage can be achieved through geographical location, multicultural neighbourhoods, mentoring, community, or social groups and activities. Prioritizing the mixed classification in foster care matching fixes mixedness as a static and unchanging identity, which relies on a deterministic and psychologizing tendency and negates the value of lived experience and cultural practices.

The Enduring Identity Question

Children's Social Care understands mixing and mixedness as a classification and experience that is confusing for practitioners and foster carers in relation to matching for placements. The literature surrounding mixedness has a tendency to underpin it as an inherent problem within the individual, rather than a problem within external, structural processes or race-making and thinking in social life. The experiences of the mixed children in this book were primarily brought about through external factors such as misrecognition, ambiguity, collapse of race, culture and ethnicity, lack of social legitimacy of mixed families, insistence that mixed children be socialized or identify with black culture, contestable racial terrain, and uncertain definition of what constitutes the boundaries of mixedness. These are structural and institutional problems, not ones inherent to the individual or to the classification, and the consequences of these assumptions create tension in the everyday experiences of mixed race children and young people in foster care.

Mixed young people in foster or residential care are particularly vulnerable to the impact of racialization and racial classification, which structure their everyday lives. The salience of race is not always a priority for mixed people (Aspinall and Song 2013; Root 1996), and further, mixed children considered other identifications such as nationality, gender, or sexuality as equally important in their lives (Ali 2003). While both these positions speak from a deconstructionist approach, they are situated and partial. Children's Social Care is a highly political site in which class and poverty, race, and gender position its users and practitioners in relationships of power. Children cared for by local authorities are now increasingly coming from mixed families, and, while race jostles for position between its deconstruction and abandonment, it still matters for groups disadvantaged by racial and ethnic classification.

The internal diversity within the mixed classification shows that often mixed people share more with other cultures than they do with each other. Defining the mixed category along racial and ethnic boundaries is made more complex as there is no shared ethnic heritage among mixed people. However, what is common to mixed people is their everyday experience of being mixed race, how they live with internal diversity, and how they perceive others understand them through appearance, ethnic and racial heritage, cultural practices, and family lineage. Mixed people answer questions of belonging through their lack of social legitimacy and come to increase their racial consciousness earlier and with more nuance than those with one heritage.

Mixed young people in foster care do not have the opportunity to play with identity within the public/private split of birth family homes, which Song (2003) suggests is one such strategy of mixedness (albeit one that is not entirely useful if the chosen identity fails to be socially recognized). The private identifications of young people in foster care are managed by practitioners' or foster carers' attempts to control how identity is expressed and bring it into line with guidelines and understandings of mixedness. Judgements about appropriate expression are routed through visual appearance, cultural practices, and performances. Mixedness is locked into specific ways of being, and its ontological status is secured by the expectations of others who rely upon visual signifiers to fix race to the body and reify its expression. The varied expressions of mixedness can be perceived as identity problems which need to be remedied, perhaps through CAMHS. Young people in foster care are shaped, defined, and restrained by the ethnically and culturally constitutive boundaries of their mixed classification, and how they are able to express their identification is subjected to official practitioner discourse disseminated through foster carers.

Stealth's story demonstrates the confusion surrounding mixedness, who can belong to the mixed category, and how that belonging is constituted. For Stealth, mixedness straddles two discourses, that of fixed categories which determine how he can understand and claim a racial classification, and that of multiple points of identifications which can shift across space and time in the sites of school, home, and foster care. He illustrates the confines within which care administration coerces specific types of identity through choice of placements, legitimate identification, and labelling. Lucy has been misrecognized as mixed through her visual appearance. She uses to her advantage discursive repertories of mixedness as sexually desirable, building social capital through her sexuality, age, and gender, but this increases her early sexualization and vulnerability. Both Stealth and Lucy show the limitations of understanding mixedness solely as an ethnic and racial category through the fixity of mixedness to the body and the lack of recognition for those with multiple heritages. However, claiming and maintaining mixedness as a choice when outside of the black/white binary is a precarious balancing act. We have to ask how mixed can be defined within a post-race politic. Can it or should it be constituted and restrained through a racial or ethnic classification, and if so how are boundaries to be drawn with increasingly diverse heritages?

Childhoods in Care: Retaining the Ordinary

Care offers a specific type of childhood in which ordinary understandings of children and young people are neither valid nor applicable to their circumstances. Over seventy thousand children are in care every year, but remarkably little is known about their lives. Separation of young people from their families entails a re-thinking of how they understand family and belonging. They have very few available resources for forming strong attachments to adults. The team around the child devolves responsibility, and despite young people having a range of adult professionals at their disposal, what they most lack is a significant one-to-one, dependable relationship with a trusted adult. Children in foster care need time to prioritize their own hobbies and interests outside of the demands of the care system as this encourages growth and independence and offers resources for adulthood.

Economies of Foster Care

The high cost of residential care makes fostering a more economical choice for cash-strapped Children's Social Care departments. It can cost over £2000 per week to keep one child in residential care (which exceeds the cost of Eton), while foster care can be bought for under £500 per week. While there are undoubtedly some carers who have a genuine capacity to offer a young person a real place in their families, those carers appear to be rare. The earning potential of all the carers involved in this book was low; they were neither highly educated nor skilled, and fostering is a career choice which offers a lifestyle that exceeds skill set and is primarily taken up by women who have poor earning potential in the labour market. Foster carers must focus on nurturing the child, not on being an administrator for the bureaucracies of the care system. If foster care is to be the first choice of departments, the recruitment, training, evaluation, and retention of good quality carers must remain a priority.

Despite mixed race children having an enduring and consistent relationship to the care system, stretching back over six decades in England, they are still not given specific consideration in legislation and policy.

Long-standing debates over whether mixed children in care are black *or* white not black *and* white, and now white and black, have been a red herring in relation to mitigating the circumstances of their care admission and subsequent adverse care experiences. The high instances of their admission point towards a misunderstanding of mixed families. Policy and legislation must take seriously the specific disadvantages white and black Caribbean or African children experience, support families with earlier intervention, tackle assumptions that misunderstand the race and gender dynamics of mixed families, and accept their visibly heterogeneous nature.

References

Ali, S. (2003). *Mixed-race, post-race: Gender, new ethnicities and cultural practices.* Oxford: Berg.

Aspinall, P. J., & Song, M. (2013). *Mixed race identities.* Basingstoke: Palgrave Macmillan.

Mills, C. W. (1959). *The sociological imagination* (reprinted in 2000). Oxford: Oxford University Press.

Root, M. P. (1996). *The multiracial experience.* Newbury Park, CA: Sage.

Song, M. (2003). *Choosing ethnic identity.* Cambridge: Polity Press.

Appendix

Name	Age at end of research	Time in Care	Classification	Current Foster Placement	No. of placements
Lucy	20	14 years	Jamaican mother and Jamaican father	Semi-Independent/care leaver	16
Amma	12	6 years	Irish mother and Ghanaian father	Jamaican carer	18
Tallulah	12	9 years	Scottish mother and Jamaican father	White British carer	2
Jasmine	14	9 years	Scottish mother and Jamaican father	Jamaican carer	3
Stealth	12	18 months	Mixed race mother (Jamaican and English) and Jamaican father	Jamaican carer/s	1

Fig. A.1 Participants—all names used are pseudonyms, chosen by the participants

© The Editor(s) (if applicable) and The Author(s) 2016   **193**
F. Peters, *Fostering Mixed Race Children*,
DOI 10.1057/978-1-137-54184-0

Bibliography

Alexander, C. (1996). *The art of being Black*. New York: Oxford University Press.

Alibhai-Brown, Y., & Montague, A. (1992). *The colour of love*. London: Virago Press.

Alleyne, B. (2001). *Personal narrative and activism*. London: Goldsmiths College.

Alleyne, B., & Alexander, C. (2002). Framing difference racial and ethnic studies in twenty-first century Britain. *Ethnic and Racial Studies, 25*(4), 541–551.

Anthias, F. (2005). Social stratification and social inequality: Models of intersectionality and identity. In F. Devine, M. Savage, J. Scott, & R. Crompton (Eds.), *Rethinking class: Culture, identities and lifestyle*. Basingstoke: Palgrave.

Appiah, K., & Gutmann, A. (Eds.). (1998). *Color conscious: The political morality of race*. Princeton, NJ: Princeton University Press.

Aspinall, P. (1996). *The development of an ethnic group question for the 2001 census: The findings of a consultation exercise with members of the 2001 census working sub group on the ethnic question*. Unpublished manuscript.

Aspinall, P. (2003). The conceptualisation and categorisation of mixed race/ethnicity in Britain and America: Identity options and the role of the state. *International Journal of Intercultural Relations, 27*(3), 269–296.

Back, L. (1996). *New ethnicities and urban culture*. London: UCL Press.

Banks, N. (1999). Direct identity work. In R. Barn (Ed.), *Working with Black children and adolescents in need*. London: BAAF.

Banton, M. (1977). *The idea of race*. London: Tavistock.

© The Editor(s) (if applicable) and The Author(s) 2016
F. Peters, *Fostering Mixed Race Children*,
DOI 10.1057/978-1-137-54184-0

Banton, M. (1987). The battle of the name. *New Community, 14*(1–2), 170–175.

Bardo, S. (1990). Feminism, postmodernism and gender scepticism. In L. Nicolson (Ed.), *Feminism and postmodernism.* New York: Routledge.

Bardo, S. (1998). Bringing body back to theory. In D. Welton (Ed.), *Body and flesh: A philosophical reader.* Oxford: Blackwell.

Bauman, Z. (2003). *Liquid love.* Cambridge: Blackwell.

Bauman, Z. (2004). *Modernity and its outcasts.* Cambridge: Blackwell.

Bebbington, A., & Miles, J. (1989a). Children who enter local authority care. *British Journal of Social Work, 19*, 349–368. Oxford: Oxford University Press.

Bebbington, A., & Miles, J. (1989b). *The background of children who are looked-after in local authority care.* London: BAAF.

Beck, U., & Beck-Gernsheim, E. (1995). *The normal chaos of love.* Cambridge: Polity Press.

Belsky, J. (1984). The determinants of parenting: A process model. *Child Development, 55*, 83–96.

Belsky, J. (1998). Paternal influence and children's well being: Limits of new direction for understanding. In A. Booth (Ed.), *Men in families: When do they get involved? What difference does it make?* Mahwah, NJ: Lawrence Erlbaum Associates.

Berger, J. (1972). *Ways of seeing.* London: Penguin.

Bhattacharyya, G. (1999). Teaching race in cultural studies. In M. Bulmer & J. Solomos (Eds.), *Ethnic and racial studies today.* London: Routledge.

Boas, F. (1940). *Race language and culture.* New York: The Free Press.

Bourdieu, P. (1979). *Distinction: A social critique of the judgement of taste.* London: Routledge.

Bradbury, B. (2003). *Child poverty: A review* (Policy Research Paper No. 20). Canberra: Commonwealth Department of Family and Community Services.

Bradford, B. (2006). *Who are the 'mixed' ethnic group?* London: Office for National Statistics.

Brah, A., & Phoenix, A. (2004). Ain't I a woman? Revisiting intersectionality. *Journal of International Women's Studies, 5*(3), 75–86.

Brown, M. (2002). *Catch a fire: The autobiography.* London: Headline Book.

Brown, N. President of the Association of Multiethnic Americans.

Browning, G. (2000). Contemporary liberalism. In G. Browning, A. Halchi, & F. Webster (Eds.), *Understanding contemporary society: Theories of the present.* London: Sage.

Brush, P. S. (2001). Problematizing the race consciousness of women of colour. *Signs, 27*(1), 171–198. The University of Chicago Press.

Bulmer, M., & Solomos, J. (1999). *Ethnic and racial studies today.* London: Routledge.

Bundi, L. (1993). Locating identity politics. In M. Keith & S. Pile (Eds.), *Place and the politics of identity.* London: Routledge.

Burchell, G., Gordon, C., & Miller, P. (1991). *The Foucault effect: Studies in governmentality.* Chicago, IL: University of Chicago Press.

Caballero, C. (2007). Mixed families: Assumptions and new approaches. In J. Sims (Ed.), *Mixed heritage identity, policy and practice.* London: Runnymede.

Caballero, C., Edwards, R., Goodyear, A., & Okitikpi, T. (2012). The complexity of the everyday lives of mixed racial and ethnic families: Implications for adoption and fostering practice and policy. Autumn/Winter, *36*(3 and 4). *Adoption and Fostering, 36*(Autumn Issue), 9–24.

Caballero, C., Edwards, R., & Smith, D. (2007). Cultures of mixing: Understanding partnerships across ethnicity. *21st Century Society, 3*(1), 49–63.

Charmaz, K. (2006). *Constructing grounded theory.* New Delhi: Sage.

Chrisitian, M. (2000). *Multiracial identity.* Hampshire: Macmillan Press.

Cicourel, A. V. (1964). *Method and measurement in sociology.* London: The Free Press.

Civitas. (2002). *Experiments in living: The fatherless family.* London: Civitas.

Cohen, P. (1999). *New ethnicities old racisms.* New York: Zed Books.

Connell, R. W. (1995). *Masculinities.* Oxford: Polity Press.

Dalmage, H. (2000). *Tripping the color line: Black-White multi racial families in a racially divided world.* New Brunswick, NJ: Rutgers.

Dalmage, H. M. (2004). *The politics of multiracialism: Challenging racial thinking.* Albany, NY: State University of New York Press.

de Certeauu, M. (1988). *The practice of everyday life.* Berkeley, CA: University of California Press.

de Vos, G. (1995). Ethnic pluralism: Conflict and accommodation: The role of ethnicity in social history. In L. Romanucci-Ross & G. A. De Voss (Eds.), *Ethnic identity: Creation, conflict, and accommodation* (3rd ed.). Walnut Creek, CA: Alta Mira Press.

Department of Health Social Services Inspectorate. (2002). Great Britain. In *Fostering for the future* (SSI report on the inspection of foster care services).

Department of Health SSI. (2002). Great Britain. In *The children act report 2001.* London: Department of Health.

Desforges, C., & Abouchaar, A. (2003). *The impact of parental involvement, parental support and family achievements and adjustments: A literature review* (Research Report No. 433). London: Department for Education and Skills.

Du Bois, W. E. B. (1999). *Souls of Black folk*. Chicago, IL: A.C. McClurg.

Duncan, S., & Edwards, R. (1999). *Lone mothers, paid work and gendered rationalities*. London: MacMillan.

Dunier, M. (1999). *Sidewalk*. New York: Farrar, Strauss and Giroux.

Edwards, R., Ali, S., Caballero, C., & Song, M. (Eds.). (2012). *International perspectives on racial and ethnic mixedness and mixing*. London: Routledge.

Edwards, R., Caballero, C., & Puthussery, S. (2010). Parenting children from 'mixed' racial, ethnic and faith backgrounds: Typifications of difference and belonging. *Ethnic and Racial Studies, 33*(6), 49–967.

Emmison, M., & Smith, P. (2000). *Researching the visual images, objects, contexts and interactions in social and cultural inquiry*. New Delhi: Sage.

Eze, C. E. (1997). *Race and the enlightenment a reader*. Cambridge, MA: Blackwell.

Farmer, E., Moyers, S., & Lipscombe, J. (2004). *Fostering adolescents*. London: Jessica Kingsley.

Fatimilehin, I. (1999). Of jewel heritage: Racial socialisation and racial identity attitudes among adolescents of mixed African-Caribbean/White parentage. *Journal of Adolescence, 22*, 303–318.

Ferguson, R. (1998). *Representing race*. London: Arnold.

Flynn, R. J., Dudding, P., & Barber, J. (2006). *Promoting resilience in child welfare*. Ottawa, ON: University of Ottawa.

Foren, R., & Batta, I. (1970). Colour as a variable in the use made of a local authority care department. *Social Work, 27*(3), 10–15.

Frankenberg, R. (1993). *White women: Race matters the social construction of whiteness*. New York: Routledge.

Fratter, J., Rowe, J., Sapsford, D., & Thoburn, J. (1991). *Permanent family placement: A decade of experience*. London: BAAF.

Frost, N., & Harris, J. (1996). *Managing residential child care*. Brighton: Pavillion.

Gaber, I. (1994). Transracial placements in Britain: A history. In I. Gaber & J. Aldridge (Eds.), *Culture, identity and transracial adoption: In the best interests of the child*. London: Free Association Books.

Giddens, A. (1990). *Consequences of modernity*. Cambridge: Polity Press.

Gilbert, N. (2001). *Researching social life*. London: Sage.

Gilbert, D. (2005). Interrogating mixed-race: A crisis of ambiguity? *Social Identities, 11*(1), 55–74.

Gill, O., & Jackson, B. (1983). *Adoption and race*. London: Batsford Academy and Educational.

Gillies, V. (2005). Working class mothers and school life: Exploring the role of emotional capital. *Gender and Education, 18*(3), 281–293.

Gilroy, P. (1987). *There ain't no Black in the Union Jack.* London: Unwin Hayman.

Goldie, P. G. (2002). *Nine lives.* London: Hodder and Stoughton.

Goulbourne, H., & Solomos, J. (2003). Families, ethnicity and social capital. *Social Policy and Society, 2*, 329–338.

Halchi, A., & Webster, F. (2000). *Understanding contemporary society theories of the present.* London: Sage.

Hall, S. (1980). *Race, articulation, and societies structure in domination in sociological theories: Race and colonialism.* Paris: UNESCO.

Hall, S. (1981). Notes on deconstructing the popular. In R. Samuel (Ed.), *People's history and socialist theory.* London: Routledge, Kegan and Paul.

Hall, S. (1992a). New ethnicities. In J. Donald & A. Rattansi (Eds.), *Race, culture, difference.* London: Routledge.

Hall, S. (1992b). *The West and the rest in formations of modernity.* Oxford: Polity Press in association with Blackwell and the Open University Press.

Hall, S. (1996). *Critical dialogues in cultural studies.* London: Routledge.

Hall, S., & Du Gay, P. (1996). *Questions of cultural identity.* London: Sage.

Haraway, D. (1997). *Modest_Witness@Second_Millenium FemaleMan©_Meets_OncoMouse™.* New York: Routledge.

Harper, F. D., & McFadden, J. (Eds.). (2003). *Culture and counselling: New approaches.* Heights, MA: Allyn and Bacon.

Hart, E., & Bond, M. (1995). *Action research for health and social care: A guide to practice.* Buckingham: Open University Press.

Haylett, C. (2001). Illegitimate subjects? Abject Whites, neoliberal modernism and middle-class multiculturalism. *Environment and Planning D: Society and Space, 19*(3), 351–370.

Higginbotham, E. B. (1992). African-American women's history and the metalanguage of race. *Signs, 17*(2), 251–274.

Hill-Collins, P. (1990). *Black feminist thought knowledge and consciousness and the politics of empowerment.* London: HarperCollins Academic.

Hooks, B. (1989). *Talking back: Thinking feminist: Thinking Black.* Boston, MA: South End Press.

House of Commons Children, Schools and Families Committee. Third report Looked-after Children 2008–09.

House of Commons Health Committee. *The Victoria Climbié inquiry report.* Sixth report of session 2002–03.

Howe, D. (2005). *Child abuse and neglect: Attachment, development and intervention*. London: Palgrave Macmillan.

Hoyles, A., & Hoyles, M. (1999). *Remember me achievements of mixed race people past and present*. London: Hansib.

Ifekwunigwe, J. O. (2004). *Mixed race studies a reader*. London: Routledge.

Ince, L. (1999). Preparing Black young people for leaving care. In R. Barn (Ed.), *Working with Black children and adolescents in care*. London: BAAF.

Jacobson, M. F. (1998). *Whiteness of a different colour: European immigrants and the alchemy of race*. Cambridge, MA: Harvard University Press.

James, C. L. R. (1980). *The Black Jacobins* (2nd ed.). London: Allison and Busby.

Karenga, M. (2002). *Introduction to Black studies* (3rd ed.). Los Angeles, CA: University of Sankore Press.

King-O'Riain, R., Small, S., & Mahtani, M. (Eds.). (2014). *Global mixed race*. New York: New York University Press.

Kirkman, M., et al. (2001). I know I'm doing a good job: Canonical and autobiographical narratives of teenage mothers. *Culture, Health and Sexuality, 3*(3), 279–294.

Knowles, C. (1999a). Race, identities and lives. *Sociological Review, 47*(1), 110–135. Oxford: Blackwell.

Knowles, C. (1999b). The symbolic empire and the history of racial inequality. In M. Bulmer & J. Solomos (Eds.), *Ethnic and racial studies today* (pp. 45–58). London: Routledge.

Kober, C. (Ed.). (2003). *Black and ethnic minority children and poverty: Exploring the issues*. London: National Children's Bureau.

Kress, G., & van Leeuven, T. (1996). *Reading images: The grammar of visual design*. London: Routledge.

Laming, Lord Herbert. (2003). *The Victoria Climbié inquiry* (Report of an Inquiry by Lord Laming. Cm. 5730). London: The Stationery Office.

Lawler, S. (2000). *Mothering the self: Mothers, daughters, subjects*. London: Routledge.

Lawler, S. (2005). Disgusted subjects: The making of middle class identities. *Sociological Review, 53*(3), 429–446.

Lewis, G. (Ed.). (2004). *Citizenship: Personal lives and social policy*. Bristol: The Policy Press in Association with the Open University.

Lloyd, I. (1998). *2001: A race Odyssey*. London: The 1990 Trust.

Lucey, H., & Reay, D. (2000). Identities in transition: Anxiety and excitement in the move to secondary school. *Oxford Review of Education, 26*(2), 191–205.

Malik, K. (1996). *The meaning of race*. Hampshire: Palgrave.

Margolin, G. (1998). Effects of domestic violence on children. In P. Trickett & C. Schellenbach (Eds.), *Violence against the children in the family and the community* (pp. 7–101). Washington, DC: American Psychological Association.

Martin Alcoff, L. (2005). *Visible identities: Race, gender and the self.* New York: Oxford University Press.

Maslow, A. H. (1943). A theory of human motivation. *Psychological Review, 50*(4), 370–396.

Mason, D. (1999). The continuing significance of race. In M. Bulmer & J. Solomos (Eds.), *Ethnic and racial studies today.* London: Routledge.

Mason, J. (2002). *Qualitative researching.* London: Sage.

Massey, D. (1993). Politics and space/time. In M. Keith & S. Pile (Eds.), *Place and the politics of identity.* London: Routledge.

Masson, J. M., Oakley, W., & Pick, M. K. (2004). *Emergency protection orders: Court orders for child protection crises: Research report.* Warwick: Warwick University.

May, T. (1997). *Social research issues, methods and process* (2nd ed.). Buckingham: Buckingham Open University Press.

McBride, J. (1996). *The color of water.* New York: Riverside Books.

McCarthy, J. R., Edwards, R., & Gillies, V. (2003). *Making families: Moral tales of parenting and step-parenting.* Durham: Sociology Press.

Mercer, K. (1990). Welcome to the jungle: Identity and diversity in postmodern politics. In J. Rutherford (Ed.), *Identity: Community, culture, difference.* London: Lawrence and Wishart.

Mishler, E. (1990). *Researching interviewing: Context and narrative.* Cambridge, MA: Harvard University Press.

Modood, T. (1988). Black, racial equality and Asian identity. *New Community, 14*(3), 397–404.

Montagu, A. (1974). *Man's most dangerous myth: The fallacy of race* (5th ed.). London: Oxford University Press.

Nakawaza, D. J. (2003). *Does anybody else look like me? A parents guide to raising multiracial children.* Cambridge, MA: Perseus Press.

Noble, M., Wright, G., Dibben, C., Smith, G. A. N., McLennan, D., Anttila, C., et al. (2004). *The English indices of deprivation.* London: Office of the Deputy Prime Minister, Neighbourhood Renewal Unit.

Nunno, M., & Rindfleisch, N. (1991). The abuse of children in out of home care. *Children and Society, 5*(4), 295–305.

Oakley, A. (1982). Conventional families. In R. N. Rapoport, R. Rapoport, & M. P. Fogarty (Eds.), *Families in Britain* (pp. 123–137). London: Routledge and Kegan Paul.

Omi, M., & Winant, H. (1986). *Racial formations in the United States: From the 1960's to 1980's*. New York: Routledge.

Oswell, D. (2002). *Television, childhood and the home: A history of the making of the child television audience in Britain*. Oxford: Oxford University Press.

Owen, C. (2005). Looking at numbers and projections: Making sense of the census and emerging trends. In T. Okitikpi (Ed.), *Working with children of mixed parentage*. Dorset: Russell House.

Page, R. (1984). *Stigma*. London: Routledge and Kegan Paul.

Pascoe, C. (2003). *Beyond identity: Mixed parentage children and their families— Implications for social work*. Goldsmith, MA: University of London.

Peters, F. (2000). *An exploration of micro-diversity at the intersection of a bi-racial theory*. Unpublished Dissertation.

Pithouse, A., & Rees, A. (2014). *Creating stable foster placements: Learning from foster children and the families who care from them*. London: Jessica Kingsley.

Potkay, A., & Burr, S. (1995). *Black Atlantic writers of the 18th century*. Hampshire: Macmillan Press.

Prewitt, K. (1987). Public statistics and democratic politics. In W. Alonso & P. Starr (Eds.), *The politics of numbers*. New York: Russell Sage Foundation.

Putnam, R. (2000). *Bowling alone: The collapse and revival of American Community*. New York: Simon and Schuster.

Raffo, C., & Reeves, M. (2000). Youth transitions and social exclusion: Developments in social capital theory. *Journal of Youth Studies, 3*(2), 147–166.

Ramdin, R. (1999). *Reimaging Britain: 500 years of Black and Asian history*. London: Pluto Press.

Raynor, L. (1970). *Adoption of non-White children: The experience of a British adoption project*. London: George Allen and Unwin.

Reay, D. (2000). Rethinking social class qualitative perspectives on class and gender. In S. J. Ball (Ed.), *Sociology of education: Major themes* (Vol. 2, pp. 990–1008). London: Routledge.

Reay, D. (2005). Beyond consciousness? The psychic landscape of social class. *Sociology, 39*(5), 911–929.

Reissman, C. K. (1993). *Narrative analysis*. Newbury Park, CA: Sage. Review, *29*(1), 53–76.

Roberts, B. (2002). *Biographical research*. Buckingham: Open University Press.

Roediger, D. (1991). *The wages of whiteness: Race and the making of the American working class*. London: Verso.

Romano, R. C. (2006). *Race mixing: Black-White marriage in post-war America*. Gainsville, FL: University of Florida Press.

Root, M. P. (1998). Experience and processes affecting racial identity development: Preliminary results from biracial sibling project in culture. *Diversity and Mental Health, 4*(3), 237–247.

Rose, G. (2007). *Visual methodologies: An introduction to the interpretation of visual materials.* Los Angeles, CA: Sage.

Rushdie, S. (1991). *Imaginary homelands.* London: Granta.

Rutherford, J. (1990). *Identity community culture difference.* London: Lawrence and Wishart.

Savage, J. S., & Crompton, R. (Eds.). (2005). *Rethinking class: Culture, identities, and lifestyle.* Basingstoke: Palgrave.

Sayer, A. (1992). *Method in social science: A realist approach* (2nd ed.). London: Routledge.

Sayer, A. (2005). *The moral significance of class.* Cambridge: Cambridge University Press.

Seabrook, J. (1991). My life in that box. In J. Spence & P. Holland (Eds.), *Family snaps the meaning of domestic photography.* London: Virago.

Seale, C. (1998). *Researching society and culture* (3rd ed.). London: Sage.

Seidler, V. J. (2006). *Transforming masculinities men, cultures, bodies, sex and love.* New York: Routledge.

Selwyn, J., & Wijedesa, D. (2011). Pathways to adoption for minority ethnic children in England—Reasons for entry to care. *Child and Family Social Work, 16,* 276–286.

Skeggs, B. (2004). *Class, self, culture.* London: Routledge.

Solomos, J. (2003). *Race and racism in Britain* (3rd ed.). Hampshire: Palgrave Macmillan.

Song, M., & Aspinall, P. J. (2012a). 'Mixed race' young people's differential responses to misrecognition in Britain. In R. Edwards, S. Ali, C. Caballero, & M. Song (Eds.), *International perspectives on racial mixing and mixedness. Relationships and resources* (pp. 125–140). New York: Routledge.

Song, M., & Aspinall, P. J. (2012b). Is racial mismatch a problem for young 'mixed race' people in Britain? The findings of qualitative research. *Ethnicities, 12*(6), 730–775.

Sontag, S. (1979). *On photography.* New York: Penguin Classics.

Spencer, J. (1997). *The new colored people: The mixed race movement in America.* New York: New York University Press.

Stanley, L. (1992). *The auto/biographical I.* Manchester: University Press Manchester.

Stanley, L., & Wise, S. (1993). *Breaking out again: Feminist ontology and epistemology.* London: Routledge.

Stein, M., & Maynard, C. (1985). *I've never been so lonely.* London: NAYPIC.

Stephens, G. (1999). *On racial frontiers.* Cambridge: Cambridge University Press.

Storr, A. (1989). *Freud: A very short introduction.* New York: Oxford University Press.

Strathern, M. (1992). *After nature English kinship in the late twentieth century Britain.* Cambridge: Cambridge University Press.

Swindells, J. (1995). *The uses of autobiography.* London: Taylor and Francis.

Thompson, P. (2008). *Doing visual research with children and young people.* New York: Routledge.

Twine, F. W. (2004). A White side of Black Britain: The concept of racial literacy. *Ethnic and Racial Studies, 27*(6), 878–907.

Twine, F. W., & Gallagher, C. (2008). The future of whiteness: A map of the third wave. *Ethnic and Racial Studies, 31*(1), 4–24.

Van Slyke, H. (1975). *The mixed blessing.* USA: Doubleday.

Wallace, K. (2004). *Working with multiracial students critical reflections on research and practice.* Greenwich, CT: Information Age Publishing.

Warren, M. D., & Johnson, W. R. (Eds.). (1994). *Inside the mixed marriage: Account of changing attitudes, patterns, and perception of cross-cultural and interracial marriage.* New York: University Press of America.

Wehrly, B. (2008). Breaking barriers for multiracial individuals and their families. *Journal of Counselling Psychology; American Psychological Association, 55*(3), 411–418.

Wertheimer, M. (2000). *A brief history of psychology* (4th ed.). Fort Worth, TX: Harcourt Brace.

Wheatle, A. (2003). *Brixton Rock* (3rd ed.). London: Black Amber Books.

Wilson, K., Sinclair, I., & Gibbs, I. (2000). The trouble with foster care: The impact of stressful events on foster carers. *British Journal of Social Work, 30*(2), 193–209.

Woolcott, H. F. (1994). *Transforming qualitative data: Description, analysis and interpretation.* London: Sage.

Wright, M. (1998). *I'm chocolate, you're vanilla raising healthy Black and biracial children in a race conscious world: A guide for parents and teachers.* New York: Wiley.

Yancey, G. (2006). Racial justice in a Black/non Black society. In D. Brunsma (Ed.), *Mixed messages: Multiracial identities in the colour blind era* (pp. 49–62). Boulder, CO: Lynne Rienner.

Zack, N. (1993). *Race and mixed.* Philadelphia, PA: Temple University Press.

Zack, N. (1996). *Thinking about race.* Belmont, CA: Wadsworth.

Websites

Department for Children, Schools and Families. www.dass.stir.ac.uk/adoption-research/study4.html (accessed on 12 May 2010).

Tapsfield, R. (2010). www.fostering.net (accessed on 12 May 2010).

The 'exoticism' of mixed race women. www.intermix.org.uk/forum/forum_posts.asp?TID=2206&PID (accessed on 15 May 2010).

www.centreforscoialjustice.org.uk (accessed on 13 November 2015).

www.intermix.org.uk (accessed on 15 May 2010).

www.ons.gov.uk/dcp171776-369571.pdf (accessed on 13 November 2015).

www.phototherapy.org.uk/ (accessed on 20 December 2008).

www.pih.org.uk (accessed on 13 November 2015).

www.proceduresonline.org (accessed on 13 November 2015).

Visual Media

Foster, M. (Director). (2001). *Monsters ball* [DVD]. Babylon, NY: Lionsgate and Lee Daniels Entertainment.

Jones, S. C. (Writer). (2000). *Storm damage.*

Mokwe, A. K. (Director). (2010). *Little baby Jesus.*

Nicholls, J. (Director). (2010). *Imagine.* BBC.

Pilkington, L. (Director). (2002). *Brown Britain* [Video]. England: Keofilms.

Index

Note: Page numbers with "n" denote notes.

© The Editor(s) (if applicable) and The Author(s) 2016   **207**
F. Peters, *Fostering Mixed Race Children*,
DOI 10.1057/978-1-137-54184-0

as participants in research, 40, 60, 61, 114–15
Children Act (UK), 9–10, 34, 85, 140–3
Children and Adolescent Mental health Service (CAMHS), 189
children looked-after data
code set for ethnic origin, 26–7
and racial and ethnic categories, 184
SSDA903, 26
children's social care
guidelines, 2, 3, 42, 68
and intervention in mixed families, 3, 5, 32, 106
policy, 12–13, 16
processes, 40, 56, 68, 84
class
dis-identification of, 39
middle class values, 11, 123, 138
and race, 2, 3, 13, 30–1
standards of parenting, 123
classification
and categories, 2, 24, 26–7, 42–3
and the Census, 24–6, 28–9
and race, 2, 13, 14, 30, 40, 42
and whiteness, 125
Cohen, P., 11, 137
community support, 176
contact
and birth family, 117–18, 176
Christmas, 116–18, 120
and siblings, 30, 101, 139–40
and social media, 152
unregulated, 180
council estates, 170
culture
black paradigm, 143

as family practice, 12, 14, 37, 73–6
and Liberal perspective, 143
as socialization, 14, 35, 68, 74, 144–5

D

Dewan, I., 13, 43, 79
diaspora
and belonging, 4, 132, 134–5, 153
difference
as biological, 57
as irreconcilable, 38, 42
as racial, 37, 167
disadvantage
of mixed race children in care, 30–1
domestic violence, 34, 106, 185
dual heritage, 77

E

education, 15–18
Personal Education Plan (PEP), 87
see also academic achievement
emotions
handling emotions, 62–3
as knowledge, 5, 8, 62–3, 92
in research, 3, 60–4
England, 3, 10, 13, 24, 25, 27, 28, 30, 34, 42, 190
see also Britain
ethnicity, 29, 75–6, 146
and matching for fostering, 14–15
and race, 14–15, 28, 44
see also visible difference

Hughes, D., 18
hypo descent, 41, 46

I

identification, 24, 80–2
  and ascription, 40
  as process, 40, 59, 68, 81
  see also labeling
identity
  commonality of, 12
  construction of mixed, 57, 77, 82
  group identity, 46
  inherent, 32, 45–6, 59–60, 81
  not recognized, 47, 77
  and physical appearance, 75
  as problematic, 23–4, 45–8
  and self-definition, 59–60
Ifekunwigwe, J.O., 44
institutions
  and bureaucracy, 77–8
  and crisis, 7, 183
interracial relationships, 144
  reasons for, 145
  see also assumptions; families

J

journeys
  through care, 134
  see also transience

K

Katz, I., 33–4, 60
Kinship care, 11, 72
Knowles, C., 35, 111
Kuhn, A., 100

L

labeling, 80–3, 89
  see also terminology
leaving care
  and motherhood, 158, 180
  processes, 159
  and semi-independent living, 2
  and sexual exploitation, 2
  and sexual vulnerability, 180
  and social capital, 174–5
  support, 2, 17, 158
  and young women, 159
Liberal paradigm, 143
Life Story work, 128n1, 130
lived experience
  as commonality, 47
  as knowledge, 5
  of mixedness, 5, 32, 40, 43–4, 59
location
  of foster placements, 15
  multi racial, 146
long-term fostering, 2, 4, 14, 39,
    100, 114–16, 124–5, 144

M

marginality, 45–6
marginal man
  and identity problems, 45
masculinity, 169, 173
Massey, D., 38, 164
McKenzie, L., 38–9
memory
  dissonance of, 100
  and loss, 101
  and siblings, 111–13
mental health, 7–8
mentoring, 187

Printed by Printforce, the Netherlands